Minor Standard Gauge Railways

R. W. Kidner

THE OAKWOOD PRESS

ISBN 085361 264 1

First published January 1981

An expanded and revised version of 'Standard Gauge Light Railways' first published 1937 and progressively revised up to the sixth edition, 1971

MINOR RAILWAYS – INTRODUCTION

A factor common to most minor standard gauge railways was more or less permanent penury. The reason for this is that undertakings which tapped an ample source of traffic were snapped up by one of the bigger lines, usually before they opened. Often however, the true potential – or lack of it – was not apparent until after traffic began, and minor railways were sometimes well-endowed to begin with, at the expense of the shareholders, who later found they had lost their money. The crunch came when this initial equipment began to wear out, and the traffic had not raised the money to pay for new equipment. At this point the purveyors of second-hand engines and carriages came into their own, these including of course the larger railways themselves, who were glad to accept £60 for a carriage or £200 for an engine which they had intended to scrap anyway. This stock was usually almost time-expired, and did not last long under its new owners, so that it was laid aside and fresh bargains sought for – thus such lines often had a great deal of stock on their books, little of which was in working order.

At the time of the passing of the Light Railways Act in 1896, which excused small lines from certain obligations such as complete signalling, there was only a handful of minor lines which had not been taken up, sometimes grudgingly, by a 'big brother'. But this Act brought forth a large crop of new minor railways, again often well-funded to start with, which again in due course found themselves in desperate straits; some were rescued by the 'Grouping' of 1923; others maintained a precarious existence up to Nationalisation, and had a few years more of existence where some local freight was worth picking up, if the overheads were reduced by making the line virtually a siding.

It is doubtful whether the 'preservation' era even if it had come earlier would have saved many minor lines, most being in areas where there was insufficient tourist traffic. The only one which has seen proper restitution is the Kent & East Sussex, now that the short-lived vintage passenger service on the Derwent Valley has ceased. There have been other minor survivals – a short section of the Tanat Valley has outlived the 'main line' complex at Oswestry to which it was attached.

The early euphoria with which some minor lines were launched often left legacies other than the waste of capital involved; the Bishops Castle, which had intended to drive to a port on the coast of North Wales to capture some Irish traffic, but which finally settled just for serving the town of Bishops Castle, was left with a junction at Lydamheath facing the wrong way, and for sixty years every train had to 'run round' there to reverse direction. The Mid-Suffolk also had a situation where its main line did not get built – this was to run from Westerfield to Halesworth – but the branch from Haughley to Kenton, and part of the main line onwards, was built. However, it stopped short at Laxfield, though the water supply for the engines was further on, along a bit of line never opened for passengers, resulting in wasted light running.

The MSLR also presents one of those fascinating conundrums as to whether certain bits of line ever were open. A short stretch of the main line from Kenton southwards was actually built and track laid – there are photos of the contractors' engine at Debenham. It seems that some local people had wagons delivered to Debenham for a time, but officially Debenham was never on the railway map. The same situation applied to the Manchester and Milford Railway, whose direct 'mountain' route to Aberystwyth was never finished, though construction was carried out to Llangurig and earthworks half a mile further. One train is recorded as having reached Llangurig before the whole section was abandoned – few railways surely can claim only one train in a lifetime. It is rather sad walking along the route of an abortive railway; the gradually diminishing earthworks show how the promoters' hopes fell and finally died. A good example is the Liskeard & Caradon line, where one can walk along the 'new line' of 1882 intended to reach Launceston, round Minions Mound to Cheesewring, observing the awkward junction with the lines to the quarries and to the Phoenix Mine, forced by earlier developments before the grand new strategy arose; then along the route of the old Kilmar Railway which would have formed part of the new main line, and finally diverge along the new construction abandoned in 1886, which after a fine granite overbridge duly completed, suddenly ends in a cutting many miles from anywhere.

The actual working methods of some smaller lines is a matter of conjecture, though it certainly included some things which would have raised eyebrows at the Board of Trade. The Wotton Tramway used chains for shunting, even in the days when it was being run by the London Passenger Transport Board. Some of the stations had a siding facing Up and no loop. Down trains with a wagon to deliver would attach a long chain between it and the train, and as the train moved forward the points would be moved under the chain – and this with passengers in the carriage. The Liskeard & Caradon also had sidings facing down the gradient and no loops; the fact that the brake-van used on the branch had a pulley just below the roof in its end bulkhead suggests that as the train went towards Cheesewring, the guard waited for the right moment as he approached the points, and then pulled something to lift the coupling hook so that the wagons could run into the siding with their own momentum after the train had passed over the junction – not too different from main-line 'slipping', but on the main lines facing points were not allowed to be moved in front of an approaching slip portion.

Another unusual practice was that of the guard climbing along the foot-boards in motion to issue tickets. This was done on the Kent & East Sussex as late as 1942 before the corridor carriages were acquired. There was also some short-cuts employed to suit the staff; for instance on the East Kent the last train into Shepherdswell often stopped by the Golgotha Tunnel, uncoupled the wagons and left them on the line for shunting next day, then uncoupled the engine which ran down to the shed, and finally the carriage (with its passengers) would glide down into the station platform under gravity and hand-brake. On the same line in its later days scheduled stops were regularly missed if no-one on the train wished to alight there, and on Down trains if there was no passenger aboard for Canterbury Road, the train would stop just beyond Wingham; the engine would enter a siding and the carriage run past it; they would then couple up and proceed back to Sheperdswell.

Propelling was also done when convenient – or sometimes from necessity. When the once-a-week service on the S&MR from Kinnerley on the Criggion branch was cut back to Melverley (due to the insecurity of the viaduct over the Severn), since there was no loop there the train had to propel, unless the Ford motor was in action.

Even though by the 'thirties many of the small lines were desperately decayed, they were not unhappy places. At Bishops Castle, where on Tuesdays, Wednesdays and Thursdays there were only two trains per day, there was plenty of time, and the driver would spend some time polishing the brass dome of 'Carlisle' so that you could see your face in it if you looked through the spectacles. He would also give a short footplate ride, even if it was during the period between trains and there was only 40 lbs. of steam in the boiler. The Manager might be busy doing something with his Sentinel steam-wagon or Berliet bus. They never had that hollow empty feeling you get at a B.R. station between trains, say at Aberystwyth after the Rheidol train has gone up the valley and the DMU has drifted off to Shrewsbury.

Take the situation at Rolvenden when the author first visited this fascinating station in 1932. It was a Friday, a fairly slack day; the staff there had to send out four trains during the day to Headcorn, three of which were in Bradshaw at 'motors' so there was no need to provide first-class accommodation. There was also four trains to Robertsbridge, two of which were supposed to be motor car workings. On the day in question both the motor sets were not working, and the 0–6–0 *Juno* was on the Robertsbridge end, and the 2–4–0T *Tenterden* on Headcorn. *Juno* had come in from the morning trip with injector trouble, and the fitter was muttering darkly about the engine's designer, perhaps not aware he had been dead for fifty years. *Tenterden* moved up to Tenterden Town for the afternoon run to Headcorn with two old Great Eastern Railway four-wheelers and a few vans and open wagons, which would snatch quite a bit at each start and stop. *Juno* was finally got operational for the afternoon run to Robertsbridge, and went up to Tenterden pushing its 'train', a single arc-roofed ex-LSW bogie compo brake. Meanwhile where was the rest of the ample stock? Of the engines, the 'Terriers' *Bodiam* and *Rolvenden* were in the two sidings alotted to derelict stock, together with the 0–6–0 *Rother*; none were complete. The steam railcar was there too, as well as the former Pickering bogie carriages and much else. The 2–4–0T *Northiam* was in the engine shed with 0–6–0ST *Hesperus;* No. 4 *Hecate* had left to join the Southern Railway, and its replacement, an LSWR 0–6–0ST, had just arrived and was in the back of the shed. On the other side of the station, in the siding alotted to 'runners' was the other LSW arc-roofed compo brake, the old 1848 LSW first saloon, and a later LSW 3rd. brake, No. 1; also a guards van, hand-crane and some open wagons. Of the petrol cars, the Shefflex was in the paint-shop (but not being painted) and the Ford was near the points at the south end, looking ready to go if required. The only item of stock not normally kept at Rolvenden, a ex-North London Railway passenger brake, was up at the Town station being used for storage. There would be some mild activity; at Rolvenden itself an old man was in the little print shop on the platform setting type for some form or other; at the manned stations other retired gentlemen would be sorting fruit-baskets and milk-churns for putting on the train, or getting out their flags to see it across the road. It was a day like any other; maybe a score of passengers would travel – but not all the way – and a bit of revenue would come in from livestock, market produce, fertiliser and so on. Ends not quite meeting, even though nothing – absolutely nothing – was spent that did not have to be.

Some items to be found in odd corners would have taken a lot of explaining if one had come upon them without knowledge of previous history. For example, behind the running shed at Kinnerley on the S&MR could be found a very small engine with wooden wheels, a horse tramcar, and a decrepit railcar of long-forgotten make, a Wolseley-Siddeley. Each represented whole chapters in history. The engine had started life as a rich man's play-thing at Kings Lynn, then was used by Colonel Stephens as an inspection car when the S&M was being built; became the motive power on the Criggion branch; was re-boilered in 1934 and ran unofficial passenger trips after service ceased; passed to the Army during the 1939-45 war, and ended up on a plinth at a Camp on Salisbury Plain. The horse-tram was part of the same story, having been secured to run with the small engine to Criggion as a normal carriage was too heavy for the Severn viaduct. The motor car was Colonel Stephens 's first essay into converted buses on the rail, having begun life as a lorry some time about 1910; he built a passenger body on to it and try it on the K&ESR and the Selsey Tramway; it was probably not in working condition when it made its journey to Wales to Kinnerley; after sitting around there for several years, the body was taken off it and mounted on the chassis of the horse-tram, to be used for the unofficial passenger trips referred to above. Finally it became a chicken house and was still in existence a short while ago.

LOCOMOTIVES

If asked what was the most suitable engine for a minor railway (or for a larger line's branch lines) one would probably answer 'the 2–4–0T'; something with 4 ft. driving wheels and 12x18 ins. cylinders, and weighing about 20-25 tons. This would have the flexibility to cope with tight curves and would also be capable of a reasonable turn of speed if required. The Sharp Stewart standard design was a good example, and this was selected for example by the Isle of Wight Railway and others. However, when it became clear that working mixed trains was to be the lot of many small lines (most *started* with the intention of running separate passenger and goods trains), the 0–6–0ST became the favourite, since it could work a heavy mixed train without slipping, handle well in shunting, and moreover there was a copious supply of them available second-hand. Their small wheels meant low speeds, but on most lines deteriorating track soon forced this anyway. It stands to reason that small lines did not look for tender engines, since their short runs did not call for much coal or water, and turntables were a luxury they were not likely to afford. Some lines did however use tender engines, the Bishops Castle (one) presumably because it was available cheap; the East Kent because they were looking for – and sometimes got – really heavy coal trains from the new mines on the route; and the Shropshire & Montgomeryshire and Kent & East Sussex because of Colonel Stephens's large purchase of the old LSWR 'Ilfracombe Goods' – a type incidentally designed for a Light Railway, which the Ilfracombe branch once was.

Two exceptions stand out from the norm: the K&ESR's 43-ton 0–8–0T 'Hecate', and the G&KER's equally heavy 2–6–0T 'Blackpool'. The former saw almost no service on its own line; there have been several explanations for its design, mainly supervised by Col. Stephens, including one that it was for a heavily-graded branch that was never built. The G&KE 1909 design was no doubt approved in the hope that the newly-extended railway would attract heavy salt traffic from the industrial branch near Knott End. However the heaviest *light* railway engines were probably the two 0–6–2Ts (nearly 50 tons) on the Plymouth Devonport & South Western. The Engineer for this undertaking was also Col. Stephens, and the decision to order these heavy engines for such a steeply-graded line was justified many years later when the S.R. tried to work the line with its E1R 0–6–2Ts and found they were not up to the job.

There were of course a number of minor railways which were worked from the first by main-line companies, especially with the rash of Light Railways after 1896. Most companies managed to find engines of a suitable character with low axle-loading and short wheelbase; the GER made good use of its tiny 'coffeepot' 0–6–0Ts, often with the leading wheels uncoupled. However both the LSWR and SECR were in difficulties, and both had to purchase 'Terrier' 0–6–0Ts from the LBSC, the first for Lyme Regis Railway and the second for the Sheppey Light. The GWR in particular had a large supply of small engines, many inherited from minor railways it had taken over and which could be switched from one line to another as required.

It might have been thought that railcars would answer many of the small railways' problems, but the capital cost of these was high compared with second-hand engines or carriages. Colonel Stephens devised his own brand of cheap back-to-back railbus, and used them on all his lines except the EKR and WCP; the latter used a Drewry car (and later purchased a bigger one from the SR) and the DVLR also had back-to-back cars for a while. The steam bogie railcars were too heavy and too long for most lines. The name of the game in running a small railway was flexibility, and this the railcar did not have; if heavy enough to haul a tail-load it was expensive to run; if light and not fitted with standard draw-gear, it was a nuisance in operation.

CARRIAGES

Some early visitors to minor railways commented on the unsuitable nature of the picture views in the carriages (not everyone may recall that in the old days all compartments sported six landscape photographs of local beauty spots) and the appearance of Yorkshire scenes in a coach on the Bishops Castle in Shropshire seemed odd. It was not in fact as simple as the fact that it was in a former Hull & Barnsley Railway carriage, for this had come via the Great Western Railway when they collected at Swindon all the oddities from the smaller South Wales railways and sold off what they could in 1922; thus the carriage had had four owners. One type of coach often met with was the ex-Mersey tunnel carriage. The Mersey sold off all its stock except one when they electrified in 1903. One batch had an interesting history. The Liskeard & Looe Railway bought some, and almost as soon as they arrived a shunting error sent six of them careering down the steep branch from Liskeard (GW station) to Coombe Junction. They stayed on the track for nearly two miles of winding gradient, ran through Coombe and on to Moorswater, where the points being set for the carriage siding, they demolished the carriage shed and most of the fairly new bogie carriages in it. However most of the Merseys survived and years later appeared on workmens trains on the GWR's South Wales lines. The history of carriages is less well recorded than that of engines; for example the two ex-LSWR saloon on the Weston Clevedon & Portishead probably came via the Plymouth Devonport & South Western and may even earlier have been in the private train of the Necropolis Company in London, but what little history is recorded became confused with the also incomplete history of two earlier LSWR Royal Saloons which ended up in Colonel Stephen's hands, one of which probably came via the PDSWJR. The subject has been fully dealt with in a companion booklet 'Carriage Stock of Minor Standard Gauge Railways'. The main-line companies most keen to sell off old stock were the North London (to 15 lines), the Mersey, LSWR, GER and LNWR, but examples from most companies could be found.

SIGNALLING

The earlier lines had a signalling system of a type which was regarded as adequate a hundred years ago; it seems likely that these primitive devices could also have been seen at that time on many main lines, but were swept away as the years passed, whereas on the minor lines they simply fell into disuse. For example on the Bishops Castle signals were set up at the end of the track at Bishops Castle and also at Lydhamheath. It has been stated that these were fixed at danger to warn the driver that he was running out of rail, but in fact they had levers and were more likely intended to show how the points were set at the far ends of the loops. The West Somerset Mineral used a very old type of disc-and-crossbar signal; the S&MR used swivelling diamond-shaped boards at minor stations to indicate if a train was to stop. On the Bideford Westward Ho & Appledore the signals were mainly used to protect road crossings; the concept of home and starting signals was rarely found; on the K&ESR one post on the platforms carried arms for each direction. These systems soon fell out of use; the staff and ticket system – and the more common fact of 'one engine in steam' – was adequate protection.

TRACK

If one wanted to know what kind of track was used in the early days of railways, one only had to look around the minor lines. The S&MR was still using track laid in 1865 for its predecessor, the 'Potteries' line; the Wotton Tramway even in LTE days could still show at the end of Church Siding a length of the light bridge rail on longditudinal sleepers dating from its horse-worked days. Everywhere, although lines on which passenger trains ran were kept in fair condition, in the sidings anything went. Standards varied enormously; the Bishops Castle used earth ballast and even on its 'main line' in its latter days inserted bisected small tree trunks to replace rotten sleepers. On the other hand, lines such as the East Kent or the South Shields Marsden & Whitburn Colliery, on which heavy coal trains had to move, needed good 90 lb. rails and sleepers at normal intervals. Most of the light railways built in the post-1896 'rush' used 56 lb. flat-bottom rail, though most of those promoted by or taken over by the large companies were re-laid before their demise.

STATIONS

The older lines had solidly-built stations as seen elsewhere, but the 1896 light railways went for corrugated iron in a big way. Some – the Sheppey Light and WC&PR for example – decided against platforms at intermediate stations, and instead fitted their carriages with steps leading to ground level; or in the case of the Great Eastern Railway light lines, special rolling stock with small wheels and low floors. Intermediate halts with no shelter at all were not unknown, and even termini often did not sport such refinements as lavatories or lighting. At the depots, sheds were usually provided for engines in use, but seldom for carriages. Wind-pumps were widely used in connection with small round water-tanks to provide a water supply free of any cost.

WAGONS AND GOODS TRAFFIC

Few minor railways had any illusions that their goods stock would be allowed over main lines, and since there would be little to move between points on a short line, not much goods stock was ordered. However, almost all lines had one or two goods brakes (little used), and some had cattle-wagons and horse-boxes. A few open wagons and box-vans were needed if only for the railway's own use. The Bishops Castle was unusual in having some iron box-vans. The Colonel Stephens lines had small inside-bearing open wagons for use with railcars, mainly for passengers' luggage.

Brake vans ceased to be used for their proper purpose early on; mixed trains usually had the wagons at the rear with no brake van. The BCR brake van was used to carry small goods; on the S&MR the Criggion stone trains often had a passenger brake at the tail.

All lines had at least one hand-crane, usually second-hand. This was employed inside the depots for assisting in engine dismantling etc. and was also moved to various sidings for lifting tree-trunks and such like. On the Derwent Valley the hand-crane (lettered No. 1) was for a time the only item of rolling stock not hired from the NER.

At one time open wagons were used to pick up hay mown on the verges; sometimes these were dropped off between stations by the last train to be loaded before the next day's first train.

Some minor railways had private sidings, to which main-line wagons were worked; in certain cases there was an established working of private owners' wagons in considerable number; for instance BQC wagons loaded at Criggion (S&MR) could be seen all over the main-line systems. The WC&PR had its own private wharf on the River Yeo; the M&MR had a wharf at Aberystwyth; the PD&SWJ served its wharf at Calstock by means of a tall wagon-lift down from the viaduct across the Tamar; the West Somerset Mineral was entirely based upon the harbour at Watchet, and had no connection with the GWR though it crossed it.

A special note is required for the Isle of Wight lines; as they had no connection with other railways (though there was a very brief wagon ferry) they needed much more goods stock than a mainland minor line, including the whole gamut of timber bolsters, tank wagons etc. An early photo shows IWCR open wagon No. 139 – whether this line really had that number of wagons is uncertain. By SR days there were only two important goods workings; one was the run from Shide chalk-pits to the Medina cement works – this was done entirely with private owner's wagons in yellow 'Blue Circle' livery. The other was coal from Medina Wharf, including a run to Ryde Gasworks – this used standard coal wagons brought over from the mainland. Brake vans (latterly ex-LSWR) were always used.

CIVIL ENGINEERING

Many light railways were laid more or less on the surface without major cuttings or embankments; with their light loading they did not fear the odd stretch of 1 in 50. They avoided tunnels; any proposed light railway needing a major tunnel would not be likely to get built, owing to the expense. However, they could not avoid crossing water, and the structures required tended to be built on the cheap and to give trouble later. The S&MR had two viaducts arcoss the Severn; the PD&SWJ an expensive one across the Tamar; the WC&P crossed the Yeo near its mouth. Even short bridges across brooks and rhines gave trouble after the timbers had been in for thirty years or so. Roads were mostly bridged by the earlier lines, but post-1896 companies had innumerable level crossings; they did not need to be gated, but had cattle-guards; the most infamous was perhaps the WC&PR one at Worle, where there were several accidents, including a tussle between the small railcar and a Bristol bus; in the end colour-light signals had to be placed there.

Part I: The "Colonel Stephens" Railways

KENT & EAST SUSSEX

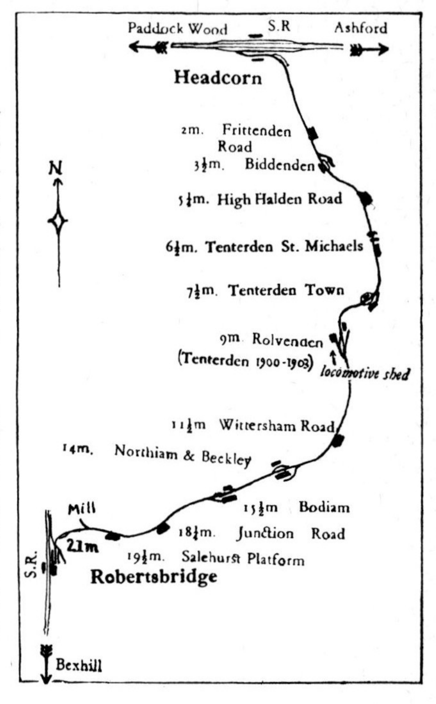

Opened as Rother Valley Railway, Robertsbridge to Rolvenden (then called Tenterden), 2/4/1900, to Tenterden 15/4/1903. Extended to Headcorn, and name changed to Kent and East Sussex 15/5/1905. Became part of B.R. (S. Region).

Closed for passengers (except hoppers' specials), and for goods between Headcorn and Tenterden Town, 2/1/1954; closed entirely by British Railways 22/4/1961, except portion Robertsbridge to Mill. Taken over by Preservation Society 1962.
Re-opened Tenterden-Rolvenden 3 Feb. 1974; to Popes Cottage May 1975; to Newmills Channel 1976; to Wittersham Road 5 March 1977.

Locomotives				*Built*
1	**Tenterden**	2-4-0T	Hawthorn Leslie (2420)	1899
2	**Northiam**	2-4-0T	Hawthorn Leslie (2421)	1899
3	**Bodiam**	0-6-0T	L.B. & S.C.R. *Poplar* pur. 1901 Ai, reb. Aix 1943	1872
4	**Hecate**	0-8-0T	Hawthorn Leslie (2587) To S.R. 949, 1932	1904
4		0-6-0ST	L.S.W.R. 0335 Beyer Peacock From S.R. 1932	1876
5	**Rolvenden**	0-6-0T	L.B. & S.C.R. *Wapping* pur. 1905	1872
6*		4-whl. steam railcar. R. & Y. Pickering		1905
7	**Rother**	0-6-0	L.S.W. (B.P. & Co., 1208) 0349 pur. 1910	1873
8	**Hesperus**	0-6-0ST	Manning Wardle 630(†)	1876
9	**Juno**	0-6-0	L.S.W. (B.P. & Co., 1210) 0284 pur. 1914	1873

*At one time No. 16 in carriage stock.

†*Ringing Rock* of North Pembroke & Fishguard Rly., became G.W.R. 1380.

No. 1 was rebuilt with 4 ft. 1 in. drivers.
No. 2 worked on the East Kent in 1923.
No. 3 became B.R. 32670: returned to K. & E.S. 11/4/1964.

All except Nos. 3 and 4 were scrapped between 1934 and 1945, in the following order: 7, 5, 6, 1, 9, 2, 8. Precise dates cannot be assigned. No. 4 scrapped 1948 by S.R.

Also Ford (1923) and Shefflex (1930) twin car petrol sets.

Coaches: Six Hurst Nelson 4-w. (two 1st, four 3rd); 1905, three Pickering bogie (reb. from 4-w.); two G.E.R. 4-w. 3rd bk. and 1st, L.S.W.R. 4-w. 3rd bk., 6-w., 1st and 3rd compo., and 1st saloon from 1848 Royal Train (purchased from P.D. & S.W.J.R.); **two NLR pass. bk., another GER set (two 3rd. bk. one 1st); three more Pickering bogie (sold); four more LSW 4w. and 6w**; 1932, two S.R. (L.S.W.) lowroof bogie. 1936, two S.R. (L.S.W.) high roof bogie; 1943, two S.R. (L.S.W.) corridor bogie (3rd and 1st bks.) 1947 one ditto.

The following S.R. locos have worked on the line:—

1936-8	0-6-0T	P Class	1556	1943	0-6-0	Oi Class	1426
1939-45	0-6-0T	Alx Class	2655	1946	0-6-0T	P Class	1325
1940-	0-6-0T	Alx Class	2678	1947	0-6-0T	P Class	1555
1940-	0-6-0	0395 Class	3440	1952	0-6-0	Oi Class	32370

The Preservation Society has acquired the following locomotives:—

10 **Sutton**	**0-6-0T**	**ex-LBSC Alx No. 50**	**1876**
11 **Dom**	0-4-0G	Ex-Jersey Eastern Rly. railcar.	
12 **Marcia**	0-4-0T	Peckett,	1923
14 **Charwelton**	0-6-0ST	Manning Wardle	1917
15 **Hastings**	0-6-0ST	Hunslet (469) ex-Sproxton Qy	1888
16	Bo-Bo	diesel-electric ex-Ford, B-TH	1931
17 **Arthur**	0-6-0ST	M & W (1601) ex-APCM	1903
18 Westminster	**0-6-0ST**	**Peckett ex-Fovant and APCM**	**1914**
19	**2-6-0**	**ex-Norwegian State R.376**	**1919**
20	railcar	ex-G.W. diesel No. 20	1940
21 **Wainwright**	0-6-0T	ex-S.R. (U.S.A.) D.S.237, Vulcan	1942
22 **Maunsell**	0-6-0T	ex-S.R. (U.S.A.) D.S.238, Vulcan	1942
23 H. F. Stephens	**0-6-0ST**	**Austerity Army 91**	**1953**
24 William Austen	**0-6-0ST**	**Austerity Army 95**	**1953**
26	**0-6-0ST**	**Stephenson & Hawthorn**	
27 Baglan	**0-4-0D**	**ex-BP Chemicals**	
28	**0-6-0D**	**Hunslet ex-Tunnel Cement**	

Railcar (4w.) ex-BR W79978 purch. from NYMR 1980.

No. 10 was originally **Gervase** O-4-OG M&W (1472) of 1900, ex-Standard Brick Merstham
No. 11 was originally **Dom** O-4-OG ex-Jersey Eastern Sentinel railcar later Standard Brick Merstham

EAST KENT

Opened in portions for goods, from 11/1912; for passengers, Shepherdswell to Wingham Col., 16/10/1916; existing sidings, Wingham Colliery to Canterbury Road, and Eastry to Sandwich Road opened to passenger traffic, 1925. Extension Sandwich Road to Richborough not open to passenger. Sandwich Road service suspended 31/10/1928. East Kent Rly., became part of British Railways (Southern Region). Passenger service ceased 30/10/1948, closed entirely Eastry-Richborough 27/10/1949, Eastry-Canterbury Road 25/7/1950, Eythorne-Eastry 1/7/1951.

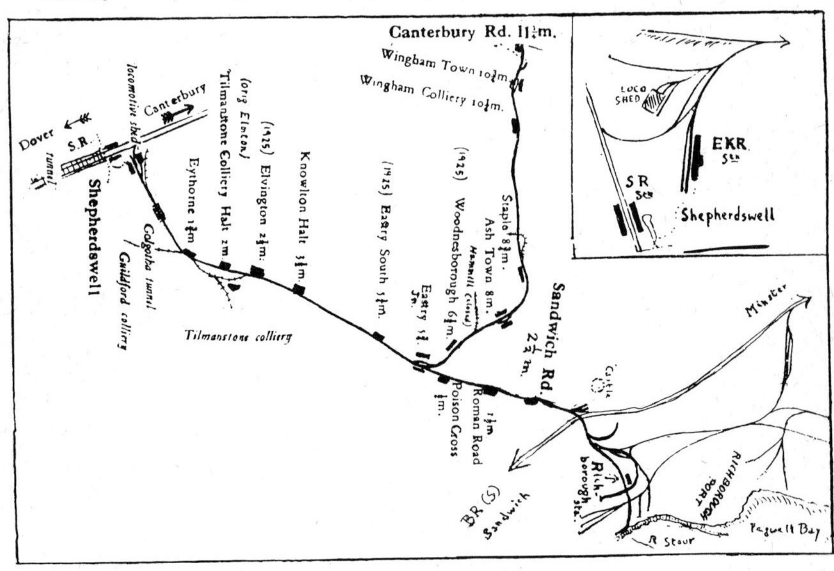

Locomotives			*Built*
1	0-6-0ST	Fox Walker 271 for Whitland & Cardigan Railway, became G.W.R. 1386, sold 1911 to Bute Docks, then also 1911 to E.K.R. Scr. 1938.	1875
2	0-6-0ST	*Walton Park* Hudswell Clarke (823). Obtained in 1916 from the S. & M.R., who had it from the W.C. & P.R. Sold 1943.	1908
2	0-6-0	No. 100 until 1946.	
3	0-6-0	L.S.W.R. 0394. Beyer Peacock, purchased 1916, scr. 1934.	1880
4	0-6-0T	Kerr Stuart 3067, purchased 1919 from Richborough Port.	1917
5	4-4-2T	L.S.W.R. 488. Neilson 6209 (purchased 1919 from War Dept., sold back to S.R. 1938).	1885

6	0-6-0	S.E.C.R. O Class. 372. S. Stewart purchased 1923, reb. with O1 boiler 1933.	1891
7	0-6-0ST	L.S.W.R. 127. Beyer Peacock (scr. 1947)	1882
8	0-6-0	S.E.C.R. O Class. 376, S. Stewart, purchased 1928, scr. 1934.	1891
100	0-6-0	S.E.C.R. O1 No. 383, S. Stewart, purchased 1935; renumbered 2, 1946.	1893
1371	0-6-0	S.E.C.R. 01 purch. 1944	1891

Line later worked by O1 0-6-0 from Dover Shed.

K. & E.S.R. *Hecate* was working at Tilmanstone Colliery in 1919; *Northiam* worked on passenger trains for a short period, in 1923.

Coaches: Originally one vestibule bogie bk.; later one C.L.C. 4-w. 3rd, three S.E.C.R. (L.C.D.) 4-w.; N.L.R. pass bk.; 4-wh. G.E.R 1st M.R. and L.S.W.R. 3rd bks.; two S.E.C.R (L.C.D.) 6-w. (2nd bk); 1945, two S.R. (L.S.W.) corridor bogie 1st and 3rd bk.

WESTON CLEVEDON & PORTISHEAD

Opened 1/12/1897 Weston to Clevedon as Weston-super-Mare, Clevedon & Portishead Tramways. Road tramway extension in Weston built 1897 but never opened. Name changed 1899 to Weston, Clevedon & Portishead Light Rly. Extended to Portishead 7/8/1907. Closed October 1940. Sold to G.W.R., used to stable wagons. Tιack removed 1942.

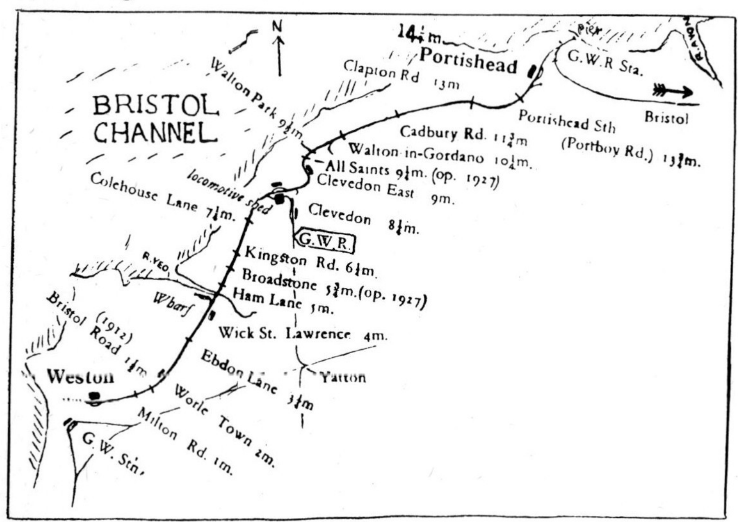

Locomotives				*Built*
	Clevedon	0-6-0T	Walker Bros., (hired?) 1897	—
	Harold	0-6-0ST	Kitson, hired 1896-7	—
1	**Weston**	2-2-2WT	Sharp Stewart ex-Furness Rly.	1857
2	**Clevedon**	2-2-2WT	Sharp Stewart ex-Furness Rly.	1866
3	**Portishead**	0-6-0T	R. Stephenson; sold to Renishaw Ironworks.	1887
	Emlyn	0-6-0ST	Kitson, hired 1903/5/7/8	—
1	**Clevedon**	2-4-0T	Dubs (1272) Jersey Rly., scr. 1940.	1875
2	**Portishead**	0-6-0T	Manning Wardle (1134), purchased 1907, sold* 1926.	1890
3	**Weston**	0-6-0ST	Manning Wardle (734), †scr. 1940.	1881
4	**Walton Park**	0-6-0ST	Hudswell Clarke (823) to S. & M.R. 1913.	1908
2	**Portishead**	0-6-0T	Aix ex-L.B.S.C.R. *Gipsy Hill*; became G.W.R. No. 5, 1940.	1877
4	**Hesperus**	2-4-0T	Sharp Stewart (2578) Watlington & P. Risboro' Rly. (G.W.R. 1384), purchased 1911, wdn. 1937.	1876
5		0-6-0ST	Manning Wardle (1970), sold 1940.	1919
4		0-6-0T	Aix ex-S.R. (L.B.S.C.R.) 2653, purchased 1937, became G.W.R. No. 6, 1940.	1875

*M. & W. No. 2 was No. 11 of Logan & Hemingway, of Doncaster, then bought by Naylor Bros., sold to W.C. & P., and resold 1926 to Wm. Cowlin, Bristol.

†M. & W. No. 3 was *Resolute* of J. M. Smith, of Bury; sold to Burry Port & Gwendreath Valley Rly., then to Ynyscedwin Colliery, then to Gabbutt & Owen of Huddersfield.

Clevedon (1), *Portishead* (1) ran as 2-4-0T, *Emlyn* as 0-4-2ST. K. & E.S.R. *Northiam* worked on the line in 1918.

2-2-0 petrol Muir-Hill Fordson engine 1925 (scrapped due to accident, 1925), 0-4-0 petrol Muir-Hill Fordson engine, 1926

Railcars: 4-w. Drewry 25/35 h.p., built 1921. 4-w. Drewry, purchased from S.R. 1934, built 1927.

Coaches: 1-6 American-type bogie cars built Lancaster Carriage Works 1897, 7-13 4-wh ex-Metropolitan Rly., 14 G.E.R. 4-wh. bk., 15-17 4-wh. L.S.W.R. vestibule. Nos. 8-13 close-coupled in pairs, 15-17 close-coupled as three-coach set.

18 ex-TVR 4w.3rd.bk.

SHROPSHIRE & MONTGOMERYSHIRE

Opened 1866 Shrewsbury to Blodwell and Criggion as Potteries, Shrewsbury & North Wales Rly. Closed 1880. Reopened Shrewsbury to Llanymynech 13/4/1911 as Shropshire & Montgomeryshire Light Rly. Criggion branch re-opened 1912. Blodwell line taken over by Cambrian Rly. Whole closed to regular passenger traffic 6/11/1933, but occasional passenger trains still ran. Taken over by Military 1941. Transferred to B.R. 1948, but remained on lease to Military. Criggion branch closed 4/1/60; remainder 29/2/60.

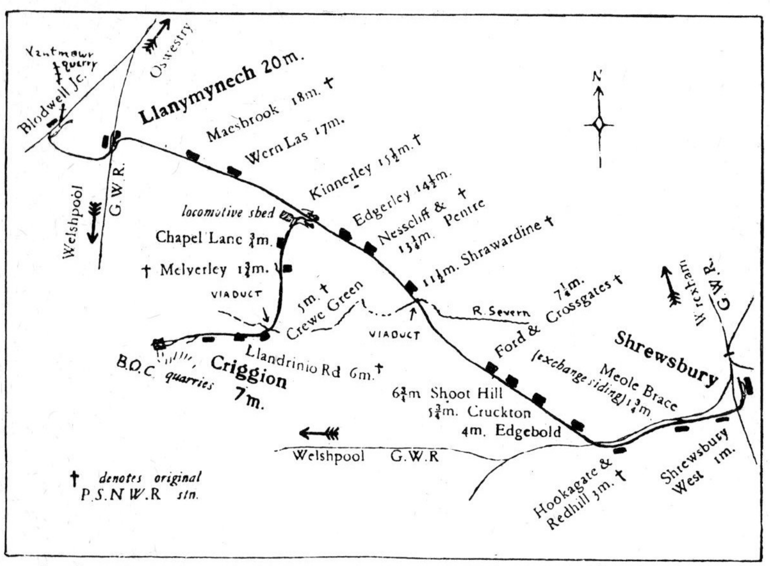

Small section of line continued in use at Hookagate in connection with BR sleeper depot

Locomotives				*Built*
1	**Gazelle**	0-4-2WT	Dodman, Lynn. Reb. from 2-2-2. Wood wheels. Purchased 1911 from T. Ward, Sheffield.	1893
2	***Severn**	0-4-2ST	Bury, as 0-4-0. **ex-Bristol Port Ry**	1853
3	**Hesperus**	0-6-0	L.S.W.R. 0324 Beyer Peacock (1517), purchased 1911, scr. 1942.	1875
4	**Morous**	0-6-0ST	Stratford & Mid. Rly. 1, purchased 1911 (to Selsey Rly.)	1866
4	**Walton Park**	0-6-0ST	From W.C. & P., 1913; to E.K.R. 1917.	
5	**Pyramus**	0-6-2T	R. & W. Hawthorn Leslie (sold)	1911
5	**Pyramus**	0-6-0	L.S.W.R. 0300. B.P. purchased 1914, scr. 1932.	1874

***Hecate** until 1921.

6	**Thisbe**	0-6-2T	R. & W. Hawthorn Leslie (sold)	1911
6	**Thisbe**	0-6-0	L.S.W.R. Beyer Peacock (1209), purchased 1916. scr. 1942.	1873
7	**Hecate**	0-6-0T	L.B.S.C.R. A1 *Beulah*, purchased 1921, scr. 1932.	1880
8	**Dido**	0-6-0T	L.B.S.C.R. A1 *Millwall*, purchased 1923, scr. 1932.	1878
9	**Daphne**	0-6-0T	L.B.S.C.R. A1 *Earlswood*, purchased 1923, scr. 1942.	1880

Unnumbered Three L.N.W.R. 1874 "coal" 0-6-0, L.M.S. Nos. 8108, 8182, 8236, purchased 1930, 1931, 1932 respectively. (8108 repainted as No. 2 1939, reverted to 8108 1942.)

Railcars: 3-car Ford (built Edmunds. Thetford). 1921: single Wolseley-Siddeley, c. 1923, **ex-KESR & WSR. Body to horse-tram frame 1935.**

All ex-S. & M. locos. scrapped by 1942 except *Gazelle*, now preserved at Bordon Camp, Hants.

W.D. Locos.: Ex-L.N.E.R. 0-6-0T 7388, 70084, 7088, 70091; ex-G.W.R. 0-6-0, 70093/6/7/8/9, 70169/70/75/76 (G.W. Nos. 2433, 2425, 2442, 2415, 2528, 2479, 2536, 2571, 2558); *Ashford* Avonside 0-6-0ST; Ruston diesel 0-4-0 72215.

Coaches: Four bogie and two 4-wh. bk. ex-M.R. and ex-London horse-tram. Later six 4-wh. ex-L.S.W.R., three ex-N.S.R. and one ex-G.E.R. 4-wh., (and saloon from 1844 L.S.W.R. Royal train).

WEST SUSSEX

Opened 27/8/1897, Hundred of Manhood & Selsey Tramway. Name changed 1924 to West Sussex Rly. (Selsey Tramway Section). Closed 19/1/1935. Equipment sold by auction, June, 1936.

Locomotives				*Built*
1	**Selsey**	2-4-2T	Peckett (681). Scr. 1936.	1897
2	**Sidlesham**	0-6-0ST	Manning Wardle (21), *Henrietta* of J. & M. Charlesworth, Leeds; later of Blagdon waterworks (purchased 1907). Scr. 1934.	1861
2	**Hesperus** (later No. 3)	0-4-2ST	Neilson ex-Plymouth, Devonport & S.W. Jn. Rly., purchased 1912 (scrapped c. 1928).	1872
2	**Ringing Rock**	0-6-0ST	Manning Wardle. Sold 1934	1883
3	**Chichester**	0-4-2T	Longbottom, Railway Foundry, Barnsley, as 0-6-0ST for G.W.R. Sold to Peckett, purchased by S. Ty. 1897, converted to 0-4-2ST by Avonside. Scr. 1913.	1847

4	**Chichester** (later 3)	0-6-0ST	Hudswell Clarke (purchased 1919).	1903
4	**Morous**	0-6-0ST	M. & W. Stratford & Mid. Rly. No. 1, transferred from Shrop. & Mont. Rly. Scr. 1936.	1866
5	**Ringing Rock**	0-6-0ST	No. 2 after 1930.	1883

Railcars: Ford twin-car, petrol, 1923. Shefflex twin-car petrol, 1928.
Coaches: Three bogie cars built 1896 by Falcon, one later by Hurst Nelson, three 4-wh. from Lambourn Valley Rly. 1910, and four 4-wh, from S.E.C.R. Two L.C.D.R. 6-wh. from S.R. 1931.

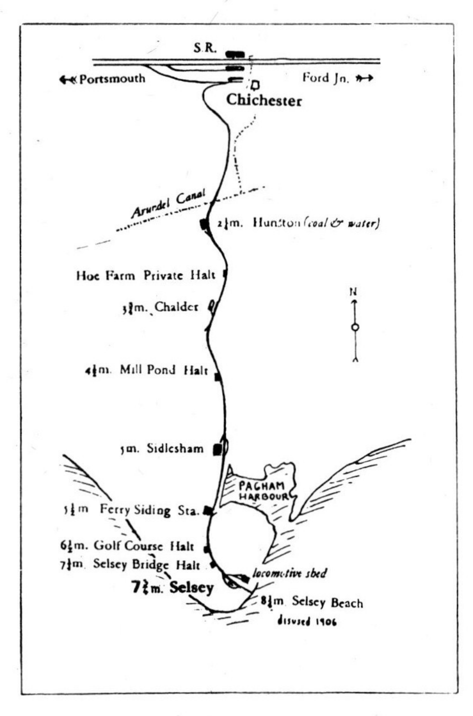

Part 2 : Other Independent Light Railways

DERWENT VALLEY

Opened 29/10/1912 Cliffe Common—Wheldrake; to Layerthorpe 21/7/1913. Closed to passenger traffic 1/9/1926. Closed entirely Cliff Common—Wheldrake 9/2/65; Wheldrake-Elvington 17/5/68. **Elvington-Dunnington closed 19 Jan. 1973**

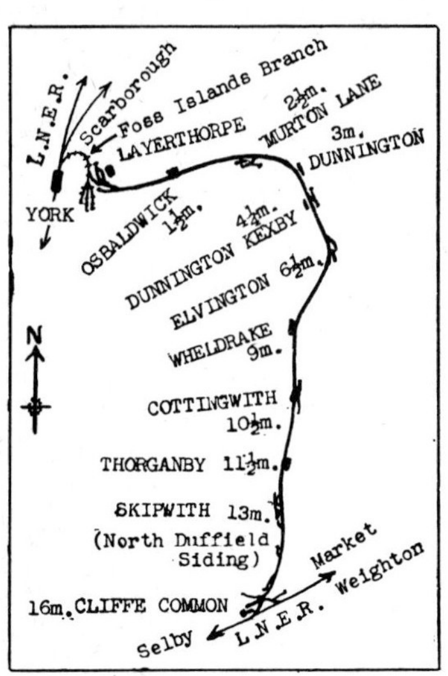

Locomotives

For the first ten years, and, afterwards intermittently power was hired from N.E.R. (later L.N.E.R. and B.R.). In 1923 an F.W.D. petrol shunter was purchased, and in 1925 a Super-Sentinel geared 4-wh. steam loco., and Ford twin-car rail-car set (all sold 1927).

Coaches: Two 4-wh. and bk., N.E.R., purchased 1913. Latterly, an ex-S.E.R. 6-wh. parcels van **(to Bluebell Ry. 1967) ex-BR Pigeon Brake**

A steam passenger service operated Layerthorpe-Dunnington 4 May 1977 to 1979, using three BR corridor coaches in blue livery

The Ford cars (sold 1927 to County Donegal Rlys.) were sometimes operated singly and light turntables were put in at Layerthorpe and Skipwith.

Ex-BR 0-6-0D 2298/2245 purch. 1969, becoming No. 1 Lord Wenlock and No. 2; BR J72 0-6-0T 69023 acq. 1977 (Joem) ex-K&WVR

EASINGWOLD

Opened 1891. Alne (N.E.R.) to 2½ m. Easingwold. 1st and 2nd class compartments only. 3rd tickets formerly issued for travel on first train of day in 2nd class compartments. Closed for passengers 29/11/1948; goods worked by B.R. (N.E.R.) loco. on loan. Closed entirely 31/12/1957. (Last train 27/12).

Locomotives		*Built*
Easingwold	Hudswell Clarke (334). Sold 1903	1891
No. 2	Hudswell Clarke (608)	1903

L.N.E.R. locos working were of J71, J72, H2 class 0-6-0T.

Coaches: Originally two N.E.R. 4 wh.; then two North London Rly. 4-wh. and one 4-wh. bk., replaced 1936 by two N.E.R. 4-wh.

Typical of an early minor railway: the Looe train standing at Moorswater station about 1890. The engine is 'Caradon' (Hopkins Gilkes 1862) and the coaches, a third, two compos and a third brake, had all been bought new (Courtesy Roger Spencer)

In this early photo of Gunnislake Station, PD&SWJR, the line's two Hawthorn Leslie 0–6–2T engines are shown; the carriages are ex-LSWR

This Rother Valley Railway train shown at Tenterden (later Rolvenden) about 1900, owes nothing to main line practice. The engine is No. 1 before it had larger wheels fitted, and the stock comprises the line's six Hurst Nelson 4w. saloons, with passenger brakes at each end

The Corringham Railway was a workmens' line, and this 1935 view of one of the two Avonside 0–6–0STs with an ex-LTSR 4w. carriage was the typical train in the line's last thirty years of working.

Plenty of polished brass on Bishops Castle Railway 'Carlisle' as it waits at Bishops Castle with the goods brake, an ex-Brecon & Merthyr compo. and ex-Hull & Barnsley brake third (Wilding & Son)

LSWR No. 127 became EKR No. 7; this photo was taken in 1935, but this 1882 engine lasted until 1941; the carriage is an ex-LCDR 6w. bk. compo (R.W. Kidner)

The East Kent purchased four of the SECR 0 class; this one, No. 6 taken in 1934, has had a short chimney fitted to enable it to work over the Canterbury & Whitstable branch (F.L. Organ)

Former BR diesel 2298 as DVLR No. 1 at Murton Crossing in 1969 (R.W. Kidner)

The type of signal used on the Headcorn Extension of the Kent & East Sussex at intermediate stations; this one is at High Halden Road (R W Kidner)

The Shropshire & Montgomery used these diamond boards at intermediate stations to indicate whether a train should stop; this is at Nesscliffe & Pentre (R W Kidner)

This unusual signal was sited at the buffer-stop end of Lydamheath station, Bishops Castle Railway (R W Kidner)

Shrewsbury (Abbey) station, S&MR, in 1929; the cylindrical water tank is just this side of the signals

Possibly the smallest station, Chapel Lane, S&MR; the wagons in the siding are B.Q.C. wagons awaiting use at Criggion (R W Kidner)

Kinnerley Junction, S&MR, in 1933. Main line ahead, with Criggion stone train in platform; carriage stock in bay; engine shed visible at left, on the Criggion branch (R W Kidner)

Rolvenden, Kent & East Sussex Railway, in 1933; left to right, Ford railcar, goods, brake and wagons, 'Rolvenden' and 'Rother' in scrap siding, ex-LSWR 4w. 3rd. bk. being painted, railcar luggage trailer in shed, No. 4 outside running shed, coal wagon and 'Northiam' in short siding with water-tank behind; afternoon train in platform (R W Kidner)

The terminus of the West Sussex Railway at Chichester; the driver is topping up the radiator of the Ford Petrol railcar set

Stradbroke Station, MSLR, shortly after opening (Loco. Pub. Co.)

Seahouses station, terminus of the North Sunderland Railway; the carriages are an ex-GER 6w. and ex-NER 4w. saloon; the loco is in the shed at the rear (Lens of Sutton)

Alexandra Docks Railway auto-train at Groeswen Halt; ex-GWR 0–4–2T No. 14 with a saloon from the Barnum & Bailey circus train (T. Gould)

The Burry Port & Gwendreath Valley Fairlie engine 'Mountaineer' (F. Moore)

One of the small Millwall Extension Railway 2–4–0Ts, running as PLA No. 31, at North Greenwich station in 1915

Colne Valley Railway; one of the 2–4–2T engines at White Colne about 1910

The PLA railway station at Gallions on 25 Sept. 1933; the engine in the foreground is William Cory's Sentinel 'Greenwich'; behind, an LNER block train of ex-GER six-wheelers with a 2–4–2T (R.W. ***Kidner)***

A typical Isle of Wight 'cocktail' at Brading about 1926; the 2–4–0T engine is ex-IWR, the first coach LC&DR 4w. converted from 6w., the second is the trailer portion of the IWC steam railcar, the third an ex-IWC 8w., converted from a Midland Railway clerestore 12w.; the van is ex-LSWR (P.H. Davison)

Freshwater Yarmouth & Newport Railway train at Newport in 1921; the 0–6–0ST engine was later SR W1 'Medina'; the carriages are ex MSJ&A Railway 'firsts', mostly demoted to 'third' (H.C. Casserley)

The Easingwold was unusual in relying on one engine only, hiring from the NER when required; this modest-sized 0–6–0ST from Hudswell Clarke replaced an earlier one from the same makers in 1903

The routes of the reservoir construction railways were rugged; this passenger train on the Elan Valley line is approaching Dol-y-Mynach in the Claerwen Valley about 1896; a 0–6–0ST engine is hauling six early GWR four-wheelers, five 2nds. and one 1st. (Severn Water Authority)

GWR 0–4–2T No. 567 was purchased by the Bishops Castle Railway in 1905; it was their only engine not named, being referred to as 'No. 1'; it is here seen at Bishops Castle in 1933 (R.W. Kidner)

Mid-Suffolk Light Railway No. 2 was built by Hudswell Clarke as a 2–4–0T 'passenger engine' but was converted as all trains became 'mixed'; it was the only one of the line's three engines to carry LNER livery after 1923.

Two of these powerful Manning Wardle engines were ordered by the Cleobury Mortimer & Ditton Priors Railway, to work passenger trains and what were expected to be heavy stone trains. Later rebuilt by the GWR as 0–6–0PTs, they lasted into BR days

Chapman & Furneaux provided the first engines for the Lambourn Valley Railway. This is the nearly-unpronouncable 'Ealhswith' at Newbury GWR about 1903. She was sold to the Cambrian Railway in 1904 (their No. 26), became GWR 820, and in 1930 went to a colliery at Radstock (F. Moore)

The oldest locomotive to be found on a light railway in the 'thirties was 'Severn' (formerly 'Hecate') of the Shropshire & Montgomeryshire. Though there have been differing stories of its origin, it seems fairly certain that it was built (possibly by Bury) in 1853 for the St Helens Railway, became LNWR 1370, and was converted to a tank engine in 1865 to become No. 2 of the Bristol Port Railway; sold by them in 1890, it worked at a colliery until being bought by the S&M in 1911. When it last ran is uncertain; this photograph was taken in July 1933; a year later only the frames and wheels were left (R.W. Kidner)

Col. Stephens's design for a light railway engine; two were built for the S&MR by Hawthorn Leslie in 1911, but both were sold shortly afterwards to the Woolmer Instruction Military Railway

The unexpected happens; in July 1934 the 41 year old 'Gazelle' of the S&MR receives a new boiler at Kinnerley (R.W. Kidner)

Colonel Stephens railways engines were scrapped in situ; this is what remains of 'Juno' at Rolvenden in June 1935

A West Sussex Railway train near Siddlesham; the engine is 'Morous', formerly Stratford & Midland Railway No. 1, and Shropshire & Montgomeryshire No. 4; the coaches are a pair of close-coupled ex-LCDR 4-wheelers

The Weston Clevedon & Portishead Railway had no platforms or buildings as some intermediate stations; here is a Portishead train stopping at Ebdon Lane 'station' in September 1936 (R.W. Kidner)

Ford railcar set on the Kent & East Sussex at Rolvenden in 1933 (R.W. Kidner)

The Nidd Valley Railway's ex-GWR steam railcar at Pateley Bridge station (F. Moore)

LNER 0–6–0T No. 7053 at Tollesbury station with two of the low-loading saloons used on the Wisbech & Upwell, K&TPR and the Stoke Ferry branch

SSM&WCR No. 7 (ex-NER) with a miners' train of GE and NB carriages near South Shields in 1936 (R.W. Kidner)

Of the five 'Ilfracombe Goods' engines bought by Col. Stephens, this was the only one that had not been rebuilt by the LSWR; No. 3 of the EKR, at Shepherdswell in 1926

Whitland & Cardigan Railway No. 2, built by Fox Walker in 1875, became GWR 1386 and in 1911 East Kent Railway No. 1; here seen in 1934 at Shepherdswell (R.W. Kidner)

The foot of the incline at Roadwater was the official limit of passenger working on the West Somerset Mineral Railway; an engine was kept at the top of the incline to work mineral trains from there to the terminus at Gupworthy

Clevedon station and depot, Weston, Clevedon & Portishead Railway, in 1936. Left, the platform; small railcar on loop line to GWR station, locomotive sheds and carriage shed (R.W. Kidner)

Shepherdswell station, East Kent Railway, in 1935. In foreground, carriage stock not in use; left hand line, two ex-LCDR 4w. and an LSWR 6w; right hand line, original bogie saloon and ex-MR 6w. Beyond, the day's train, a wagon and ex-LCDR 6w. coach; locomotive depot on left; on sky-line, empty coal wagons for the collieries (R.W. Kidner)

S&MR ex-Midland Railway goods brake No. 1 in 1934 after a rough shunt at Kinnerley (R.W. Kidner)

Mid-Suffolk Light Railway four-plank open wagon No. 4 (Loco. Pub. Co.)

BISHOP'S CASTLE

Opened 1/2/1866. Fell into Receiver's hands 1866. Closed and reopened 1867 and 1877. Closed 20/4/1935.

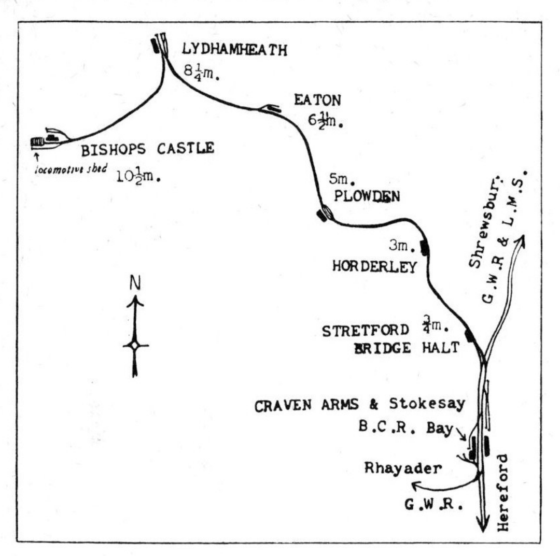

Locomotives			*Built*
Bee	0-4-0ST		—
Plowden	0-6-0	ex-St. Helens Rly., sold 1874	—
Perseverance	0-4-2T	Dodds, Rotherham, as 0-4-0 ex-Newport, Hereford and Abergavenny Rly., West Midland Rly., and G.W.R. Purchased 1870. Sold 1887 to Wrexham, Mold & Connah's Quay Rly. (Scr. 1895).	1854
Progress	2-4-0	George England. Purchased from S. & D.J.R., Scr. 1905.	1861
Bishops Castle	2-4-0	George England. Purchased from S. & D.J.R., Scr. 1905.	1861
No. 1	0-4-2T	ex-G.W.R. 567. Purchased 1905.	1869
Carlisle	0-6-0	Kitson (1421) Purchased 1895.	1868

The last two only were surviving in 1936, and were broken up. G.W.R. 107 (Fairbairn 1854 2-4-0) hired c. 1900.

Coaches: Originally three 4-wh., sold to Golden Valley Rly.; then up to 1924, six L.N.W.R. 4-wh. with chain-brake. Then one L.S.W.R. 6-wh. (1st, 2nd, 3rd class and guard compo.), one Hull & Barnsley 4-wh., and one Brecon and Merthyr 4-wh., all purchased from G.W.R.

WEST SOMERSET MINERAL

Opened by Brendon Hill Ore Co. for goods, 28/9/1859; extended to Gupworthy 1863; leased by Ebbw Vale Steel, Iron & Coal Co., 1864; opened for passengers, 4/9/1865. Closed entirely 7/11/1898. Reopened for mineral traffic Watchet-Brendon, 4/7/1907, by Somerset Mineral Syndicate. Closed 1909. Watchet-Washford section used in 1911 for signalling experiments by A. R. Angus Ltd. Land sold 8/8/1924.

Permission to open the stations above Coombe Row was refused; however, passengers were conveyed at their own risk as far as Brendon. Above incline a Neilson 0-4-0ST was used.

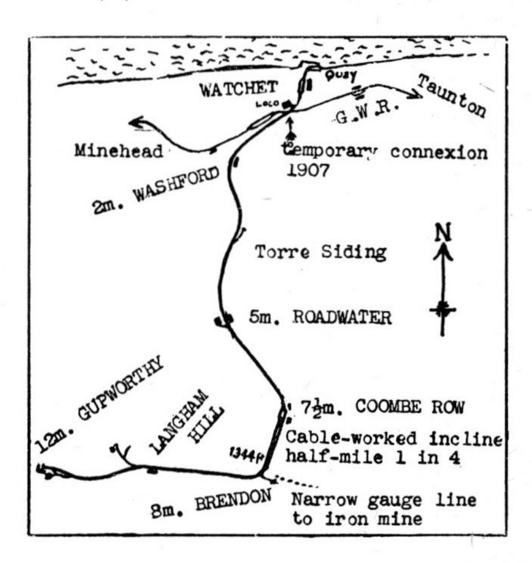

Locomotives			*Built*
Two Neilson	0-4-0ST	built 1854/61.	
Esperanza	0-6-0ST	Neilson	1854
Rowcliffe	0-6-0ST	Sharp Stewart	1857
Brendon	0-6-0ST	,, ,, ...	1857
Atlas	0-6-0ST	,, ,, sold to South Hetton Coal Co.	1865
Pontypool	0-6-0ST	Sharp Stewart	1865

When reopened 1907: 4-4-0T ex-Metropolitan Rly., No. 37.

Coaches: Four 4-wh. (three sold 1898, one left derelict).

SPURN POINT

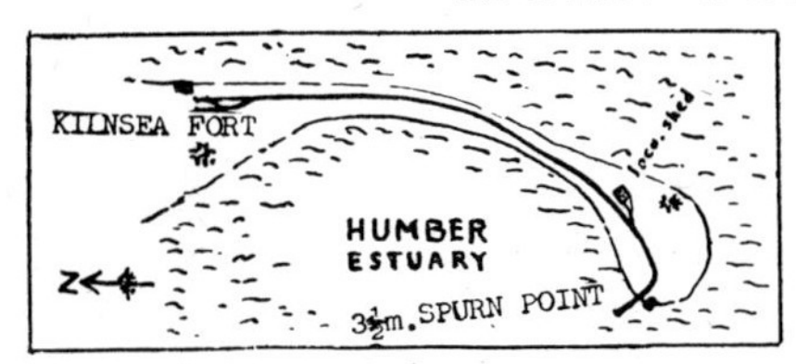

Opened about 1910. Passenger service run for crew of lighthouse and naval installations. Used for Service leave parties 1939-45. Closed entirely 1951.

Kenyon 2-4-0ST built 1888 Vulcan F. as 0-6-0ST; scr. 1929
Itala-engine railcar c.1910; Hardy railcar 1929; Hudswell Clarke railcar 1933. One coach: ex-NLR 4w.

NIDD VALLEY

Opened 11/9/1907, in connection with Bradford water supply project. Closed to passenger traffic 31/12/1929. Entirely 1936

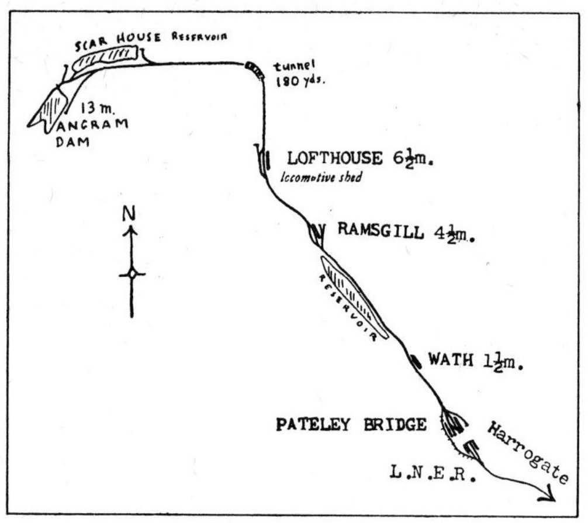

Locomotives			PASSENGER	*Built*
1	**Holdsworth**	4-4-0T	ex-Metropolitan Rly. 20 (scr.).	1866
2	**(Milner)**	4-4-0T	ex-Metropolitan Rly. 34 (sold N. Wales Granite)	1869
	Milner	0-6-0T	Hudswell Clarke (882)	1909
	Hill	Bogie	steam railcar, purchased from G.W.R. 1921 (Kerr-Stuart).	1905
			GOODS	
	Haig	0-6-0ST	Manning Wardle (1224)	1890
	Allenby	0-6-0ST	,, ,, (1379)	1898
	Beattie	0-6-0ST	,, ,, (1669)	1905
	Kitchener	0-6-0ST	Peckett (939)	1902
	Ian Hamilton	0-6-0ST	Hudswell Clarke (480)	1898
	Mitchell	0-6-0ST	,, ,, (1280)	1916
	Watson	0-6-0ST	,, ,, (1197)	1916
	Craven	0-4-0ST	,, ,, (1411)	1920
	Blythe	0-6-0ST	Avonside	1922
	Gadie	0-6-0ST	Andrew Barclay (1866)	1925
	Trotter	0-4-0ST	,, ,, (1810)	1925
	Stringer	0-4-0ST	,, ,, (1877)	1925

Coaches: First class, ten Metropolitan Rly. 4-wh.; third and workman, twelve Maryport & Carlisle Rly. 4-wh. Private saloon (Hurst Nelson) sold 1910.

NORTH SUNDERLAND

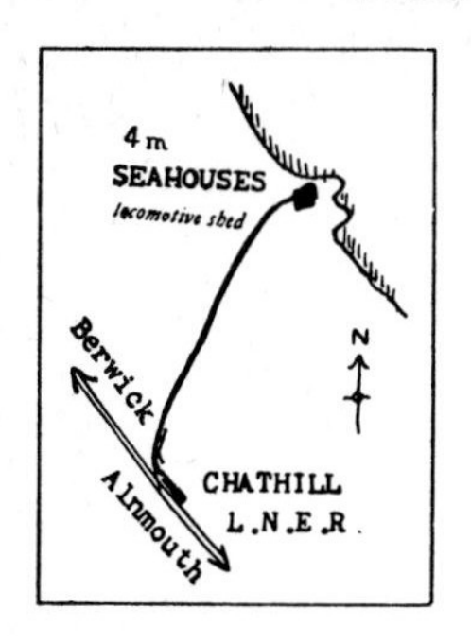

Opened 1/8/1898 (goods: passenger 11/12). Line closed 27/10/51.

Locomotives			*Built*
Bamburgh	0-6-0ST	Manning Wardle (1394)	1898
—	0-4-0	Diesel, Armstrong-Whitworth ...	1934

Also worked by L.N.E.R. Sentinel, ex-L. & Y. 0-4-0T 11217, Y7 0-4-0T 68089.

Coaches: Originally five Highland Rly., 4-wh., replaced 1916 by two N.E.R. 4-wh. and 4-wh. bk., later three G.E.R. 6-wh.

CORRINGHAM

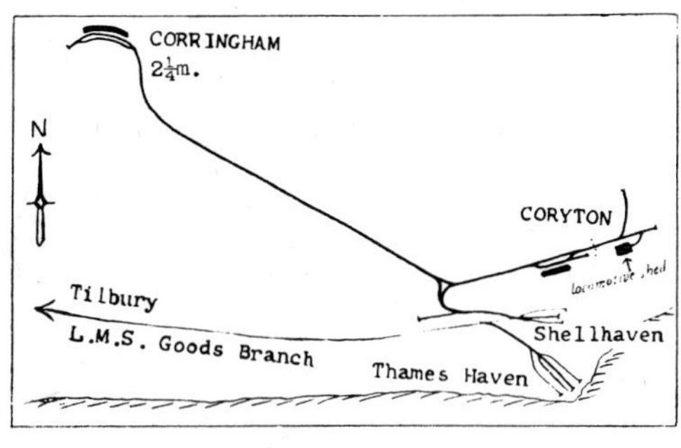

Opened 1901, from Kynochtown (goods 1/1, passenger 29/6), name changed to Coryton, 1921. Closed 2/3/1952. Main part now siding for Mobil Oil Co.

Locomotives			*Built*
—	0-4-0WT	Kitson, from Barry Rly. ...	1893
Kynite	0-4-2T	Kerr Stuart (692)	1900
—	0-6-0ST	Avonside	1914
—	0-6-0ST	Avonside, purchased 1919 ...	1917

Coaches: Originally two bogie, one open-sided, by Kerr Stuart, and one ex-L.T.S.R. 4-wh. During war a total of 12 coaches. By 1937, two L.T.S.R. 1896 4-wh. only.

SOUTH SHIELDS MARSDEN & WHITBURN COLLIERY

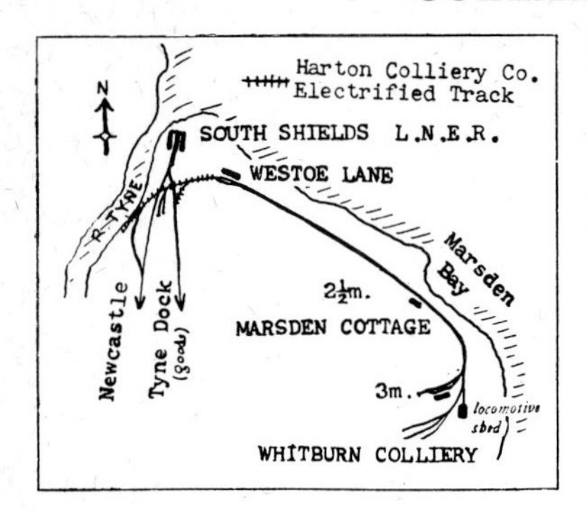

Opened for mineral traffic by Harton Colliery Co., 1870. Diverted 8/1926 by new coast road, and order obtained to work as light railway, Westoe Lane to Whitburn Colliery. Line closed 21/11/1953.

Locomotives			*Built*
1	0-4-0T	Manning Wardle, scrapped 1896	1876
2	0-6-0ST	Black Hawthorn, scrapped	1880
3	0-6-0ST	,, ,, sold	1883
4	0-6-0ST	,, ,, ,, ...	1883
5	0-6-0ST	R. Stephenson, scrapped	1887
5	0-6-0	N.E.R. 398 class, purchased '29	—
6	0-6-0	N.E.R., purchased '07, scrapped	1872
6	0-6-0	N.E.R. No. 1486, scrapped 1936	1884
6	0-6-0	N.E.R. J21 1509	—
7	0-6-2T	Chapman & Furneaux, sold to Pontop and Jarrow Rly.	1898
7	0-6-0	L.N.E. J21 No. 1616, purchased '30 ...	1892
8	2-2-2WT	Furness Rly., scrapped	1864
8	0-6-0	N.E.R. 718, scrapped	1870
8	0-6-0	L.N.E. J21, purchased '31	1889
9, 10	0-6-0	N.E.R., ex-Blyth & Tyne, scrapped 1913	—
11	0-4-0ST	Manning Wardle, scrapped 1920	—
Laleham		0-6-0ST Andrew Barclay, borrowed from Boldon Colliery 1929-38 ...	1923

No. 9, ex-W.D. Hunslet 0-6-0ST; 10, 7132, ex-W.D. Stephenson & Hawthorn 0-6-0ST; 7603, 7695, ditto 1949, 1951.

Ten electric locomotives purchased between 1907 and 1913, worked portion west of Westoe Lane (Nos. E1, E2, E10 were 4-wh., rest 8-wh.).

Coaches: About fourteen 4-wh. from G.E.R., N.B.R. and G.N. of S.R.

BIDEFORD WESTWARD HO! & APPLEDORE

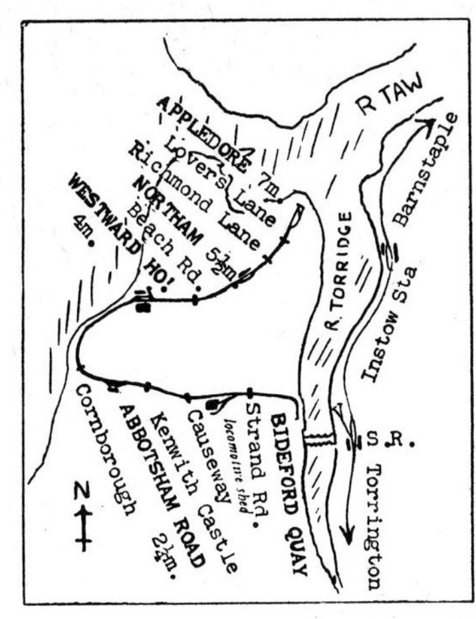

Opened 18/5/1901, Bideford—Northam, to Appledore 1/5/1908. Closed 28/3/1917 and dismantled.

Locomotives

Grenville, Torridge, Kingsley, 2-4-2T, Hunslet built 1896 (motion enclosed).

Coaches: Six American-type bogie cars, one pass. bk., vacuum-fitted, acetylene lit.

MID SUFFOLK

Opened 20/9/1904 for goods, Haughley-Laxfield, extended to Cratfield 1906. Branch unofficially open Kenton-Aspall Road, Debenham 1903 only. Passenger traffic Haughley-Laxfield 20/9/1908. Cratfield extension closed 2/1912. Line absorbed in L.N.E.R. 1923; closed 26/7/1952.

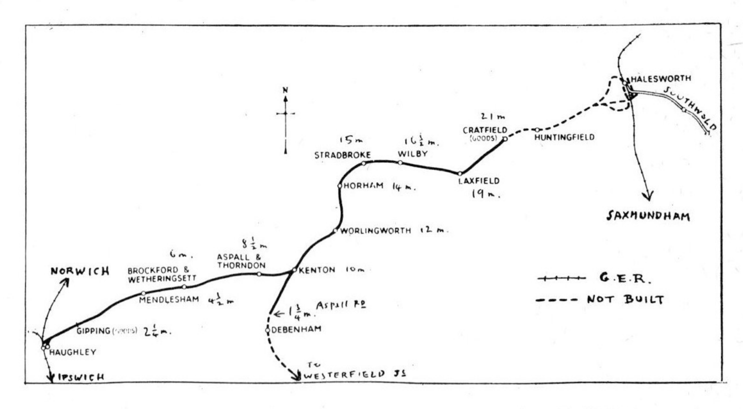

Locomotives					*Built*	*L.N.E.R.*	*Scr.*
1	0-6-0T	Hudswell Clarke	(711)	...	1904	1316	1924
2	0-6-0T	,, ,,	(723)	...	1905	1317	1928
3	0-6-0T	,, ,,	(867)	...	1909	1315	1929

No. 1 was named **Haughley** when delivered. No. 2 built as 2-4-0T.

Worked after grouping by J65 0-6-0T 7153, 7157, 7156, 7253, 7257; J15 0-6-0 65388, 65447, 65459, 65467.

Coaches: Originally **6** ex-Met. District 4-wh. Later ex-G.E.R. 6-wh.; bogie coaches used on through trains to Stowmarket.

CLEOBURY MORTIMER & DITTON PRIORS

Opened for goods 1/7/1908, for passengers 19/11/08. Grouped in G.W.R. 1923. Closed for passengers 24/9/1938. From 1956, worked for goods by R.N.A.D. with own diesel locomotive.

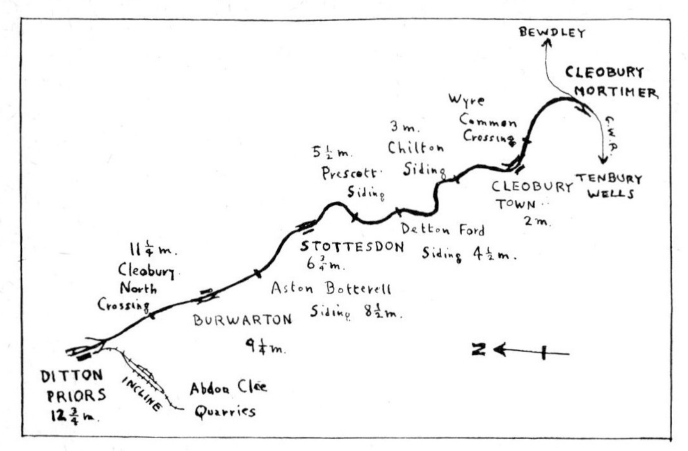

Locomotives			*Built*	*G.W.R.*	*Scr.*
Cleobury	0-6-0ST	Manning Wardle (1735)	1908	28	1953
Burwarton	0-6-0ST	Manning Wardle (1734)	1908	29	1954

Rebuilt by G.W.R. as 0-6-0PT.

Also worked briefly: ex-B.P.G.V.R. No. 8, ex-Ll. & M.M. *Ravelstone*. Abdon Clee extension worked by private locos.

Coaches: Originally four ex-N.L.R. 4-wh. rebuilt as vestibule. Later G.W.R. 4-wh.

PLYMOUTH, DEVONPORT & SOUTH WESTERN JUNCTION

Opened 2/3/1908 using most of East Cornwall Minerals Rly. (3 ft. 6 in.). Grouped in S.R. 1923. Closed Gunnislake-Callington 5/11/66.

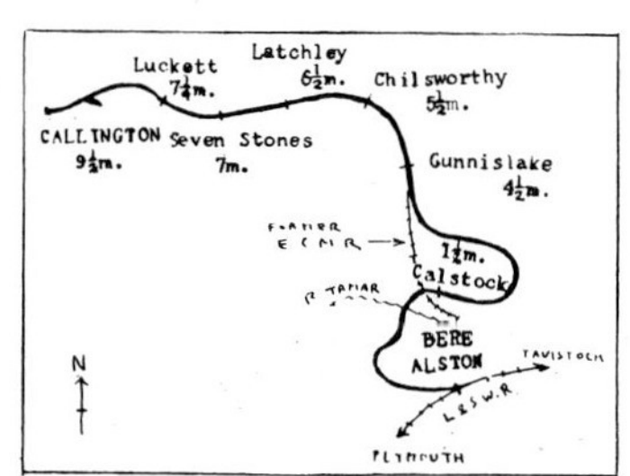

Locomotives			*Built*	*S.R.*
—	0-4-2ST	Converted from E.C.M.R. Neilson 0-4-0ST ... sold to Selsey Ty.	1872	—

A. S. Harris	0-6-0T	Hawthorn Leslie (2696)	1907	E756
Earl of Mount Edgcumbe	0-6-2T	Hawthorn Leslie (2696)...	1907	E757
Lord St. Levan	0-6-2T	Hawthorn Leslie (2695)...	1907	E758

Passenger services worked after grouping by ex-L.S.W. 02 0-4-4T, latterly by standard 2-6-2T and from 1964 by diesel.

Coaches: Originally 16 second-hand ex-L.S.W. and N.L.R. **Then four LSWR bogie (sold back to SR)**

GARSTANG & KNOTT END

Opened 14/12/1870, Garstang & Catterall—Pilling, as Garstang & Knot-End Railway (official: trains actually ran from 5/12) and closed 4/1872. Goods traffic restarted 23/2/1875, passengers 17/4. Extension to Knott End opened 29/7/1908 by Knott End Railway, which absorbed G.K.E. Grouped with L.M.S. in 1923; closed for passengers 29/3/1930; Knott End-Pilling closed entirely 13/11/50, Garstang Town-Pilling 31/7/1963.

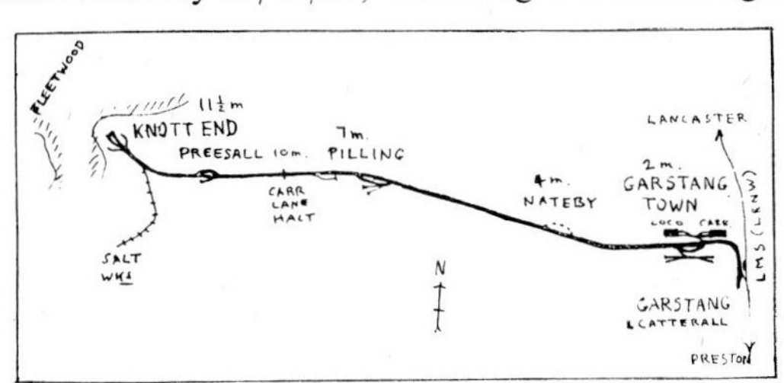

Locomotives			*Built*	*L.M.S.*	*Scr.*
Hebe	0-4-2ST	Black Hawthorn ...	1870	—	*
Union	0-4-0ST	Manning Wardle ...	1868	—	*
Farmers Friend	0-6-0ST	Hudswell Clarke & Rogers.	1875	—	*
Hope	0-6-0ST	Hudswell Clarke ...	1885	—	*
Jubilee Queen	0-6-0ST	Hudswell Clarke ...	1897	11300	1925
New Century	0-6-0ST	Hudswell Clarke ...	1900	11301	1925
Knott End	0-6-0	Manning Wardle ...	1908	11302	1924
Blackpool	2-6-0T	Manning Wardle ...	1909	11303	1924

*Hired and returned.

After grouping, L. & Y. 0-6-2T, L.N.W.R. 0-6-0 and ex-L.N.W. steam railcar. Latterly, standard B.R. 4-6-0.

Coaches: Originally four 4-wh.; eight bogie saloon; two ex-Mersey Rly. 4-wh. bought but not used; two 4-wh. passenger bk. From 1920 to 1930, only ex-L.N.W. steam railcar used for passengers, except outside excursions.

PART 3

STANDARD GAUGE LIGHT RAILWAYS OWNED OR WORKED BY MAIN LINE RAILWAYS

AMESBURY & MILITARY CAMP LIGHT. Opened 1/10/1901 from Newton Tony Junc. (2½m. W. of Grateley L.S.W.R.)—1¼m. Newton Tony—4¾m. Amesbury. For passengers 2/6/1902. Ext. 1915 to Larkhill Camp, Rolleston Camp, Fargo, Stonehenge and Druids Camp, removed 1923. Extended 1/6/1906 to 6m. Bulford Camp. Owned and worked by L.S.W.R. with standard stock; closed 30/6/1952.

AXMINSTER & LYME REGIS LIGHT. Opened 23/8/1903, from Axminster (L.S.W.R.)—4¼m. Combpyne—6¾m. Lyme Regis. Purchased by L.S.W.R. 1/1/1907, and always worked by it. Locos.: mainly Adams 4-4-2T (in 1949 Nos. 33125/488/520).

BANKFOOT LIGHT. Opened 5/3/1906 for goods, 14/5/1906 for passengers, from Strathord Jc. (C.R.) to 3m. Bankfoot. Closed for passengers 1931, goods 7/9/1964. Owned and worked by Caledonian Rly.

BARTON & IMMINGHAM LIGHT. Opened 5/12/1910 Killingholme—Immingham (Western Jetty) (1¼m.) and 3/7/1911 from Junction ½m. S. of Goxhill (G.C.R.)—2¾m. East Halton—5½m. Killingholme. Worked by railmotors in early years, later by standard stock; in later years by ex-G.N.R. 4-4-0. Owned and worked by G.C.R. Closed 17/6/63.

BASINGSTOKE & ALTON LIGHT. Opened 1/6/1901, from Basingstoke (L.S.W.R.)—3m. Cliddesden—6½m. Herriard—9¼m. Bentworth—14¼m. Alton. Owned and worked by L.S.W.R. Closed 1/1/1917 and rails taken up. Relaid and reopened 18/8/1924. Passenger service withdrawn 12/9/1932, and closed between Bentworth and Alton, closed entirely 1/6/1936. Locos.: Adams 0-4-4T, 4-4-0 and 0-6-0.

BRILL TRAMWAY. (Also called Oxford & Aylesbury Tramroad and Wotton Tramway). Opened 1/4/1871 Quainton Rd. (Met.) to near Wotton, and 1872 to Brill. Reconstructed 1894, with stations at 1¼m. Waddesdon Rd.—1¾m. Westcott—3¾m. Wotton—5m. Wood Siding—6¼m. Brill. Worked by Met. Rly. from 1/12/1899 and by L.P.T.B. on its formation. Closed 30/11/1935. Locos.: two 0-4-0 geared Aveling & Porter 1872, 0-4-0WT Bagnall 1879, *Huddersfield* No. 1 0-6-0ST M.W. 1878, *Brill* No. 2 0-6-0ST M.W. 1894, *Wotton* No. 2 0-6-0ST M.W. 1900, *Brill* No. 1 (Brill No. 2 rebuilt), and latterly by Met. Beyer Peacock 4-4-0T. Coaches: originally a short 4w. saloon, 1894 one light bogie, later Met. rigid 8w.

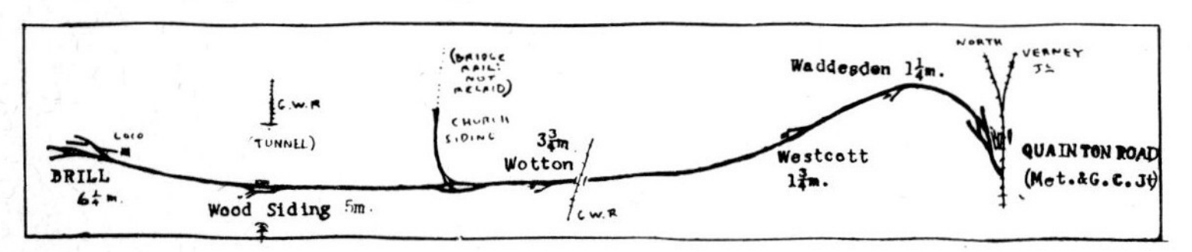

BURRY PORT & GWENDREATH VALLEY. Opened 7/1869 from Burry Port to Pembrey (embodying earlier Kidwelly & Llanelly and Pembrey Harbour tramroads) for goods only; extended 1891 from Burry Port to join the Llanelly & Mynydd Mawr Rly. at Sandy Gate. Reconstituted as light rly. and opened for passengers 2/8/1909 from Burry Port—1½m. Pembrey Halt—3¼m. Pinged Halt—5m. Trimsaran Rd.—6m. Glyn Abbey—8m. Pontyates—9m. Pothenry—11m. Pontyberen—13m. Cwm Mawr. Goods only branches served Kidwelly, Trimsaran, Cauwog, Ffoy and Rhyd-cerrig. Incorporated in G.W.R. 1922. Locos.: *Lizzie* and *Gwendreath*, 0-4-0ST T. Hughes 1868; *Mountaineer* 0-4-4-0T Fairlie 1870; *Victoria* 0-6-6-0T Fairlie 1873; *Kidwelly* and *Cwm Mawr*, 0-6-0ST Fox Walker 1872; *Burry Port* 0-6-0ST M.W. 1872; *Dyvatty* and *Pontyberen* 0-6-0ST Peckett 1891. Replaced by: 1, *Ashburnham* 0-6-0ST Chapman & Furneaux 1891; 2, *Pontyberen*, 3, *Burry Port*, 4, *Kidwelly*, 5 *Cwm Mawr*, 6 *Gwendreath*, 7 *Pembrey*, 0-6-0ST Avonside 1900-07; 8 *Pioneer*, 9, 10, 0-6-0T Hudswell Clarke 1909-11. Carriages: 19 ex-Met. Rly. 8w. and Six ex-L.S.W.R. 6w. Later standard G.W. cut-down roofs. Closed for passengers 20/9/1953.

CAIRN VALLEY. Opened 1/3/1905 from Cairn Valley Jc. (1¼m. N.W. of Dumfries G. & S.W.R.)—3¾m. Irongray—6¾m. Newtonards—7¾m. Stifford—10m. Dunscoe—13m. Crossford—14m. Kirkland—17m. Moniaive. Worked by G. & S.W.R. Closed for passengers 1/5/1943. Closed entirely 4/8/1947. Worked by G. & S.W. steam railcars at first, later by Manson 0-4-4T 269 and latterly standard types.

CULM VALLEY. Opened 12/5/1876, Tiverton Jc. (G.W.R. [B. & E.R.])—2¼m. Coldharbour Halt—2¾m. Uffculme—5m. Culmstock—6¼m. Whitehall Halt—7¼m. Hemyock. Worked by G.W.R. Locos.: two 0-6-0ST, later two ex-West Cornwall 2-4-0T, and standard 0-4-2T. Closed passengers 9/1963.

DORNOCH LIGHT. Opened 2/7/1902, The Mound (H.R.)—1¼m. Cambusavie Platform—3¾m. Skelbo—5½m. Embo—7¾m. Dornoch. Worked by Highland Rly. Closed 13/6/1960. Locos.: *Dornoch*, Stroudley 0-6-0T No. 56; later class O 0-4-4T.

ELLIOTT JUNCTION & CARMYLLIE LIGHT. Opened for goods 1854 Carmyllie Quarries—Dublin & Arbroath Rly. (worked by D. & A. from 1865 by S.N.E.R.; 1866 became part of C.R., 1897 became joint with N.B.R.)—for passengers 1/2/1900, Elliott Jn. (N.B. & Cal. Jt.)—1¼m. Arbirlot—2m. Cuthlie—3½m. Denhead—5m. Carmyllie. Closed for passengers 2/9/1929, goods 24/5/1965. Two companies worked alternate years (C.R. '172' class 4-4-0T, N.B. 4-4-0T No. 110).

ELSENHAM & THAXTED LIGHT. Opened 1/4/1913, Elsenham Jc. (G.E.R.)—1m. Mill Rd. Halt—1¾m. Henham Halt—3m. Sibley's—4½m. Cutlers' Green Halt—5½m. Thaxted. Locos.: J69 0-6-0T. Closed for passengers 15/9/1952 and for goods 1/6/1953.

FRASERBURGH & ST. COMBS LIGHT. Opened 1/5/1903, Fraserburgh (G.N. of S.R.)—1m. Kirkton Bg. Halt—$2\frac{1}{4}$m. Philorth Bg. Halt—$3\frac{1}{2}$m. Cairnbulg—$5\frac{1}{4}$m. St. Combs. Locos.: G.N. of S. 0-6-0T with cow-catchers; later D51 4-4-0T and F4 2-4-2T. Recently diesel railcar. Closed 3/5/1965.

GIFFORD LIGHT. Opened 14/10/1901, Ormiston Jc.—2m. Pencaitland—$3\frac{1}{2}$m. Saltoun—$5\frac{1}{2}$m. Humbie—$9\frac{1}{4}$m. Gifford. Leased and worked by North British Rly. Closed to passengers 3/4/1933, goods 2/5/1960. Locos.: D51 4-4-0T, later J24 0-6-0T.

GOOLE & MARSHLAND LIGHT. Opened 1901 for goods and 11/8/1903 (as Axholme Joint Rlys.) for passengers, from Marshland Junc. (2m. S. of Goole on N.E.R. line)—$5\frac{3}{4}$m. Reedness Junc.—$8\frac{3}{4}$m. Crowle Town; branch from Reedness Junc.—3m. Eastoft Halt—$4\frac{1}{4}$m. Luddington—$5\frac{1}{2}$m. Fockerby; extended 2/1/1905 from Crowle to 13m. Belton—$14\frac{3}{4}$m. Epworth—$17\frac{3}{4}$m. Haxey Town—$19\frac{1}{2}$m. Haxey Junc. (G.N. & G.E. Jt.). Epworth —($2\frac{3}{4}$m.) Hatfield Moor branch (goods only) opened 5/1/1909. Worked first by N.E.R., then by L. & Y.R. with standard 0-6-2T and 0-6-0. Passenger service withdrawn 17/7/1933. Closed Epworth-Haxey Jc. 1/2/1956. Belton-Epworth and Fockerby branch out of use by 1970.

GRIMSBY & DISTRICT LIGHT. Opened 1908 from Grimsby West Marsh Jc. to new dock under construction at Immingham. Passenger service provided by railmotors, withdrawn on opening of the Grimsby & Immingham Light on 22/7/1912, an electric (500v. overhead) line, largely laid alongside former line, from Grimsby Corporation Bridge—Yarborough St.—Stortford St.—Spencer St.—Cleveland Bridge—Immingham Town, extended 7/1913 to $5\frac{3}{4}$m. Immingham Dock. Electric line worked by 40 and 60-seat single-deck cars; steam line (now goods only) by standard stock. Both owned and worked by G.C.R. G.I.L.R. closed 3/7/1961; workmen's service reinstated on G.D.L.

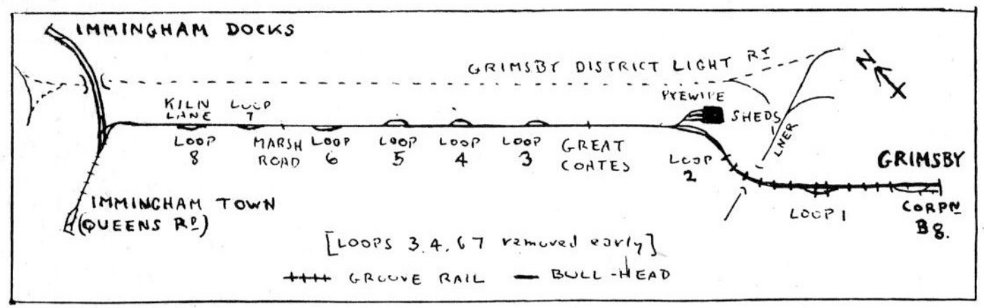

KELVEDON, TIPTREE & TOLLESBURY PIER LIGHT. Opened 1/10/1904, Kelvedon (G.E.R.)—$\frac{3}{4}$m. Brooklands Siding—$2\frac{3}{4}$m. Inworth—$3\frac{1}{2}$m. Tiptree—$4\frac{1}{4}$m. Tolleshunt Knights—$5\frac{3}{4}$m. Church Siding—$6\frac{1}{2}$m. Tolleshunt D'Arcy—$7\frac{3}{4}$m. Old Hall Siding—$8\frac{1}{2}$m. Tollesbury, extended 1907 to $9\frac{3}{4}$m. Tollesbury Pier. Locos.: J67 0-6-0T. Coaches: 6w. rebuilt as vestibule; from 1928 ex-Wisbech & Upwell 4w. and bogie, low-loading with balcony ends. Line closed for passengers 7/5/1951; Tudwick Rd.—Tollesbury Pier closed 29/10/1951 and entire line 1/10/1962.

During 1939-45 war, portion beyond Tollesbury Sta. taken over by W.D., who employed four locos. on the branch serving mobile guns. Track on Pier itself removed 1940.

Lambourn Valley. Construction begun in 1873 and again in 1883, but stopped; finally opened 4/4/1898, Newbury (G.W.R.)—1¾m. Speen—2¾m. Stockcross—4¾m. Boxford—6¼m. Welford Park—8¼m. Great Shelford—10m. East Garston—11m. Lastbury—12½m. Lambourn. Became Light Rly. 1903. Purchased by G.W.R. 1905. Locos.: *Eahlswith* and *Aelfred* 0-6-0T Chapman & Furneaux 1898, *Eadweade* 0-6-0T Hunslet 1903 (all sold to Cambrian becoming Nos. 26/35/24). From 4/1904 worked by G.W.R. steam railcars, later by diesel railcars and ex-M.S.W. 2-4-0 1334/5. Carriages: 4 light 4w., later standard. Closed for passengers 4/1/1960. Track N. of Welford Park lifted 1962.
Welford USAF siding closed 3 Nov. 1973

Lampeter, Aberayron & New Quay Light. Opened 1/6/1912 from Junc. 1½m. N. of Lampeter (G.W.R.)—½m. Silian Halt—2½m. Blaenplwyf Halt—4¾m. Talsarn Halt—5¾m. Felin Fach—8¼m. Ciliau Aeron Halt—9m. Crossways Halt—10¾m. Llanerch Aeron Halt—12m. Aberayron. Owned by G.W.R., and worked with railmotors and auto trains. Closed for passengers 7/5/1951, goods 5/4/1965 Felin Fach—Aberayron.

Lauder Light. Opened 2/7/1901, Fountainhill (N.B.R.)—6½m. Oxton—10½m. Lauder. Leased and worked by North British Rly. Closed for passengers 12/9/1932, goods 1/10/1958. Locos.: D51 4-4-0T; latterly J67 0-6-0T with empty tanks and tender.

Leadhills & Wanlockhead Light. Opened 1/10/1901 from Junc. ½m. S. of Elvanfoot (C.R.)—5¼m. Leadhills and extended 1/10/1902 to 6¾m. Wanlockhead. Closed 31/12/1938. Locos.: originally light 0-4-4T No. 72 with "cow-catchers"; later standard; coaches standard, also ex-G. & K.E.R. saloon.

Lee-on-Solent. Opened 12/5/1894 from Fort Brockhurst (L.S.W.R.)—Elmore—Browndown—Fort Gomer—3m. Lee-on-Solent. Closed for passengers 1/1/1931, for goods 29/9/1935. Worked by L.S.W.R., later S.R. Locos.: 21 *Scott* 2-4-0T G. England 1861; 392 *Lady Portsmouth* 0-6-0ST M.W. 1892; later 0-4-0T 743, P class 0-6-0T and Di class 0-4-2T. Carriages: two light bogie, later standard.

Liskeard & Caradon. Opened 1844, Moorswater Canal Basin—6½m. Caradon Mines, with horse traction. Extended 1846 to Cheesewring, 1849 to 7m. Gonamena and 1859 to 8m. Tokenbury; 1860 **to Tokenbury and 12m. Kilmar; 1882 Tokenbury-Serjeants Corner on uncompleted Launeston line.**
Line from Moorswater to Looe opened 27/12/1860 for goods, 11/9/1879 for passengers. Steam power 1862. Taken over by G.W.R. 1/1/1909. Now worked only between Coombe Junction

(nr. Moorswater) and Looe, trains running to Liskeard *via* G.W.R. loop from Coombe Junction, opened 15/5/1901. Stations (from Liskeard): 2m. Coombe Jn.—3¾m. St. Keyne—5m. Causeland—6½m. Sandplace—8¾m. Looe. Locos.: *Caradon* 0-6-0ST Hopkins Gilkes (138) 1862; 1311 *Cheesewring* 0-6-0ST Hopkins Gilkes (195) 1864; 1312 *Kilmar* 0-6-0ST Hopkins Gilkes (264) 1869; *Looe* 0-6-0T R. Stephenson 1901; 1308 *Lady Margaret* 2-4-0T A. Barclay 1907 (ex-P.L.A. No. 11). Latter standard 2-6-2T Diesel m/u from 1961. **Carriages originally four 4w; 1901 3 bogie; then 13 Merseys, from 1910 GWR.**
Looe Quay line closed, lifted 1956.

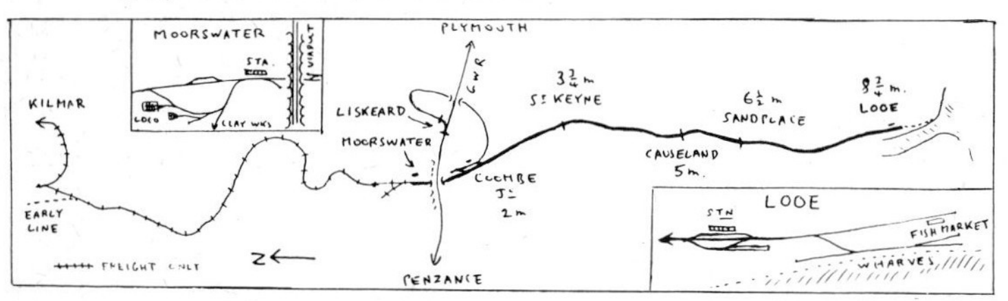

Lowca Light. Opened **1885** Rosehill Jc., (Cleator & Workington Jc. Rly.) to Lowca and Harrington Ironworks. Passenger service from 2/6/13, stations at Copperas Hill, Micklam, Lowca; ceased 6/26, workmens service to 1930, then minerals only. Line controlled by Workington Iron & Steel Co., but passenger service worked by ex-Furness S. Stewart 0-6-0's, ex-C. & W.J.R. No. 5 *Moresby Hall* Stephenson 0-6-0ST 1890, 6 *Ponsonby Hall* Stehpenson 0-6-0ST 1896.

Maidens & Dunure Light. Opened 16/5/1906, Alloway Junc. 2¼m. S. of Ayr (G. & S.W.R.)—¾m. Alloway—4m. Heads of Ayr—5¾m. Dunure—8¾m. Knoweside—11¾m. Glenside—13m. Maidens—14½m. Turnberry—19m. Girvan. Owned and worked by G. & S.W.R. Locos.: 0-4-4T 220/1, later standard types. Closed for passengers Alloway Jn.-Maidens 1/12/1930, reopened 4/7/1932, closed 31/5/1933; Girvan-Turnberry section closed for passengers 16/12/1942. Alloway Jn.—Heads of Ayr open for Butlin's traffic until 14/9/1968.

Mawddwy. Opened 1/10/1867. Cemmaes Rd. (C.R.)—1¾m. Cemmaes—Aberangell 4m.—5¾m. Mallwyd—6¾m. Dinas Mawddwy. Closed to passengers 17/4/1901, entirely 8/4/1908. Reopened as Light Railway, worked by C.R. 29/7/1911, grouped with G.W.R. 1922, closed to passengers 1/1/1931, entirely 1/7/1951. Locomotives: originally two 0-6-0ST, *Mawddwy* (M. & W. 1867), *Disraeli* (M. & W. 1868). Coaches: five 4w. ex-L.N.W. and N.L.R. Later, C.R. 2-4-0 and G.W.R. 0-4-2T, with standard 6w. stock. After 1930 various engines worked goods traffic.

North Devon & Cornwall Junction Light. Opened 27/7/1925, Torrington (S.R.)—1¾m. Watergate—4½m. Yarde Halt—5¾m. Dunsbear Halt—8m. Petrockstow—10¾m. Meeth

Halt—$12\frac{3}{4}$m. Hatherleigh—$17\frac{3}{4}$m. Hole—$20\frac{1}{2}$m. Halwill Junc. (S.R.); track of Torrington and Marland mineral line (3 ft. gauge, 1880) used between Torrington and Dunsbear. Locos.: Adams 4-4-0 and 0-6-0, later 0-6-2T specially rebuilt from Stroudley E1 class 0-6-0T. Carriages: ex-L.S.W.R. rail-motor trailers. Since 1958 B.R. Ivatt P.2 2-6-2T with standard corridor coach. Closed 1/3/1965 passengers, and goods Halwill-Meeth.

NORTH LINDSEY LIGHT. Opened 3/9/1906 from junc. 1 m. E. of Scunthorpe (G.C.R.) to 6m. West Halton-Winterton, extended 15/7/1907 to $8\frac{1}{2}$m. Wintringham and 1/12/1910 to 11m. Whitton. Worked by G.C.R. with standard stock. Closed 13/7/1925.

PONTELAND LIGHT. Opened South Gosforth (N.E.R.)—$7\frac{1}{2}$m. Ponteland, for goods 1/3/1905, passengers 1/6/1905. Extended 1/10/1913 to Darras Hall, and privately for minerals to 16m. Kirkheaton Colliery. All closed to passengers 17/6/1929; goods 2/8/1954 Darras Hall, 14/8/1967 Ponteland; still open Callerton-Gosforth Jc.

SHEPPEY LIGHT. Opened 1/8/1901, Queenborough (S.E.C.R.)—$1\frac{1}{2}$m. Sheerness East—$2\frac{1}{2}$m. East Minster-on-Sea, $3\frac{1}{4}$m. Minster—$4\frac{1}{4}$m. Brambledown Halt—$5\frac{1}{2}$m. Eastchurch—7m. Harty Road Halt—$8\frac{3}{4}$m. Leysdown. Worked by S.E.C.R. and purchased by them 31/10/1905. Locos.: ex-L.B.S.C.R. Ai 0-6-0T and S.E.C.R. steam railcar. Later P 0-6-0T and R 0-4-4T. Carriages: two articulated twin-sets. Closed 3/12/1950.

TANAT VALLEY LIGHT. Opened 5/1/1904, from junction $3\frac{1}{2}$m. S. of Oswestry—1m. Porthywaen—$2\frac{1}{2}$m. Blodwell Junc. (with disused P.S. & N.W.R.)—$3\frac{1}{4}$m. Llanyblodwell—$4\frac{1}{4}$m. Glanrafon—$5\frac{3}{4}$m. Llansilin Rd.—$7\frac{1}{4}$m. Llangedwyn—$9\frac{1}{4}$m. Pentrefelin—$10\frac{1}{2}$m. Llanrhaidr-Mochnant—12m. Pedair Ffordd—$13\frac{1}{4}$m. Penybontfawr—16m. Llangynog. Owned and worked by Cambrian Rlys. Locos.: various light tanks, latterly G.W.R. 1196/7 and ex-Liskeard & Caradon 2-4-0T 1308. Line closed to passengers 31/1/1951, and goods Llanginog-L-Mochnant 1/7/52, remainder 6/1/1964.

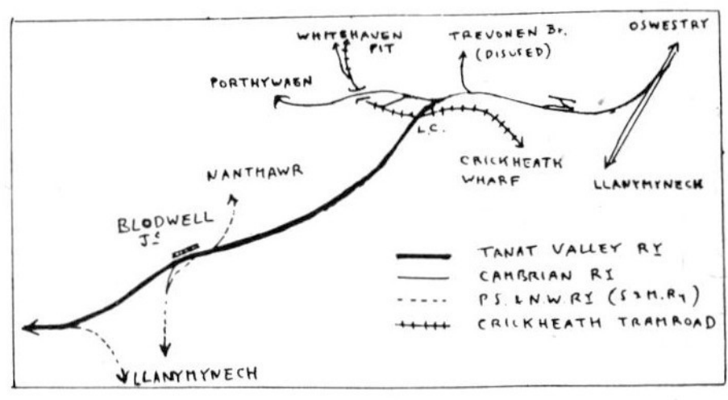

TOTTON HYTHE & FAWLEY LIGHT. Opened 20/7/1925, Totton (S.R.)—$3\frac{1}{2}$m. Marchwood—$6\frac{1}{2}$m. Hythe—8m. Cadland—$9\frac{1}{2}$m. Fawley. Owned and worked by S.R. Standard stock. Closed passengers 14/2/1966.

WICK & LYBSTER LIGHT. Opened 1/7/1903, Wick (H.R.)—4½m. Thrumster—7¼m. Ulbster—9½m. Mid Clyth—12¼m. Occumster—13½m. Lybster. Closed for passengers 1/4/1944, goods 1/2/1951. Locos.: H.R. 0-4-4T No. 13, and 4-4-0T *Olnos*; later class O 0-4-4T (during 1939-45 War S.R. Stroudley 0-4-2T).

WISBECH & UPWELL TRAMWAY. Opened 20/8/1883, Wisbech (G.E.R.)—1½m. Elm Depot—3¼m. Boyce's Depot—4m. Outwell Basin—Extended 8/9/1884 to 4¾m. Outwell Village 5m. Upwell. Owned and worked by G.E.R. Closed for passengers 1/1/1928. Locos.: 0-4-0T 130-2 (1883), 128/9 (1885), 125-7 (1891), 133/4 (1897); 0-6-0T 125-131 and 135-9 (1903-21); all enclosed-motion tram-engines. Carriages: light bogie and 4w. saloons with steps (no platforms). Later diesel loco. Closed 20/5/1966.

WRINGTON VALE LIGHT. Opened 4/12/1901, Congresbury (G.W R.)—3m. Wrington—3½m. Langford—4¼m. Burrington—6¾m. Blagdon. Closed for passengers 14/9/1931. Locos.: 2-4-0T 1384 (later sold to W.C. & P.), standard 0-4-2T. Closed entirely Wrington-Blagdon 1/11/1950.

Part 4: Shorter Notes on Some Other Minor Railways

ALEXANDRA DOCKS & RAILWAY: open for passengers from Caerphilly to Pontypridd from 31 Dec. 1897, having taken over the Pontypool Caerphilly & Newport opened for passengers 28 Dec. 1887; (this service taken over by GWR 1899). This line, one of the smallest of the South Wales lines, was merged with the GWR in 1922. It is of interest because of the varied nature of its rolling stock; the locomotives included 3 ex-Mersey 0–6–4Ts and 7 Mersey 2–6–2Ts; two steam railcars were operated, and coaching stock included three ex-Merseys and three saloons which had been part of the Barnum & Bailey circus train, one of which was operated as a rail-motor with an ex-GWR 0–4–2T (No. 14). The 37 locos were a varied collection, mostly industrial tanks, but also including three early ex-LBSC engines and three from the LNWR dating back to 1848.

CARDIFF RAILWAY: another small South Wales line, which started a passenger service from Cardiff to Rhýdyfelin as late as 1 March 1911, also using two steam railcars with trailers; carriage stock was meagre, four ex-Hull & Barnsley 4w. However in 1920 the two steamcars were converted to provide two more bogie trailers.

COLNE VALLEY & HALSTEAD RAILWAY: this was very much in 'light railway' style though opened as early as 1860 (partial); extended to Haverhill in 1863. It went to the LNER at Grouping and was closed in 1965. There were latterly only five engines: 1 0–4–2T Neilson 1877; 2 'Halstead' 2–4–2T Hawthorn 1887, 3 /2–4–2T 'Colne' Hawthorn 1887, 4 'Heddingham' 2–4–2T Hawthorn 1894, 5 0–6–2T Hudswell Clarke 1908. These replaced some rather unsatisfactory early purchases: three small 2–4–0Ts and an LBSC Sharpie 2–2–2T of 1849; also three of the earliest of the famous Manning Wardle 0–6–0STs, maker's Nos. 34/59/61 (1861-3). Carriage stock included one half of the experimental Met/Met-District six-coach electric train of 1901, demotored.

FRESHWATER YARMOUTH & NEWPORT: this Isle of Wight line opened 1888 was extremely light, and was originally worked by the IWCR. However after a dispute regarding station premises at Newport, two engines and twelve ex-MSLR 4w. 'firsts' were bought in 1913. Later a small Drewry 4w. railcar was purchased to run special parties to meet the Yarmouth boats; this survived to become a departmental trolley for the SR. Engines: 0–6–0ST M&W 1555 of 1902; 2 0–6–0T ex-LBSC No. 46. This latter was a much-travelled engine, having been sold by the LBSC to the LSWR for its Lyme Regis branch; after its FYN service it became SR W2 and later W8, returned to the main-land, became BR 32646, was sold in 1964 to the private owner of the Droxford-Fareham branch, then sold by him in 1966 to Brickwoods brewery to act as an inn-sign outside their 'pub' at Hayling, and finally rescued from there recently for further use by a preservation society.

ISLE OF WIGHT RAILWAY: this was the first railway in the Island, opened in 1864, and involved the most lucrative route, that from Ryde to Shanklin and Ventnor. Of its eight locomotives, seven were of the 2–4–0T type, and it was very much a passenger railway. Most of the coaches were four-wheelers bought new, but when the Metropolitan Railway sold off its steam stock after electrification, the IWR made a large purchase of its rather odd rigid eight-wheelers; these lasted into SR days, and their bodies (or most of them) still exist as a line of bathing huts at Brading. After the building of the steamer pier at Ryde (jointly owned with the LBSC and LSWR) traffic became really heavy and by Grouping the Ventnor route was suffering from shortage of both engines and carriages, made good by the SR with 02 class 0–4–4Ts and bogie carriages of LCD and LSW origin, so that by 1930 most of the IWR locos and stock had gone. The final fate of this line was that by 1967 it was electrified as between Ryde and Shanklin and worked by former London Transport tube stock, all other lines having closed.

ISLE OF WIGHT CENTRAL RAILWAY: a somewhat uneasy amalgamation in 1887 of the Cowes & Newport, Ryde and Newport, and Isle of Wight (Newport Junction) Railways; it had no very profitable routes, and worked its complex system with a strange collection of engines, two from the C&N, two from the R&N, one IOW (NJ), one from the North London, one Stratford & Midland, one North Eastern, four ex-LBSC – and two new. Carriage stock (total 52) was equally varied, with examples from the North London, Midland, LSW, Great Eastern – and two new. One steamcar was also acquired, and as usual it became a bogie trailer. The Southern put in the same locos and stock as they did on the IWC, but when in 1966 the last portion, the Cowes-Newport section, was closed, it was the end of the old IWC. Both the IWR and IWC were relaid by the SR with heavy chaired track, and the signalling system was brought more or less up to mainland standard – very necessary when one realises that in their heyday you could get a train from almost any station either way every half hour – and mostly on single lines!

The IWR and IWC like most minor railways had capable but small workshops at Ryde and Newport respectively; in S.R. days Ryde (St. Johns Road) became the senior, and was responsible for many practices not seen on the mainland; every engine was named, and almost all had 'Caledonian' hooters instead of whistles. Livery (all were green) was smart, and stations were well kept; here was the 'minor railway' at its best – helped admittedly by finance from the Group, and by the fact that until the introduction of the roll-on car ferries there was little motor competition.

LLANELLY & MYNYDD MAWR: this was really a colliery line, opened in 1883 and only carrying workmen passengers. Details of stock are meagre; it is known that between 1913 and 1919 nine ex-Metropolitan 4w. carriages were in use. The lines passed to the GWR in 1923.

LIVERPOOL OVERHEAD: this was hardly a railway, more an overhead tramway. It was electric from the start (1893), with 1/2nd. composite bogie cars run in pairs. Voltage was 500, and a ground-rail pick up was used. There was one steam engine; a light Kitson 0–4–0WT built in 1893 and used for moving stock in the depot. The cars were only 41/44 ft. long, and some trains of the L&YR used on a through service to Seaforth over the line from 1906 were equally short. In 1916 some 1st trailers were purchased and trains were then three-coach, 3rd/1st/3rd.

MERSEY: this line almost all in tunnel opened from Liverpool Central to Birkenhead on 1 Feb. 1886. There were 97 4w. carriages, three classes, run in 7-coach sets. The 18 engines comprised 9 0–6–4T by Beyer Peacock and 9 2–6–2Ts by Kitson, all condensing; later two ex-Metropolitan 4–4–0Ts were purchased for maintenance trains and these remained in use after electrification in 1903, though the rest were sold, 10 going to the ADR. One, 'Cecil Raikes' enjoyed a much longer life at Shipley Colliery. All the coaches except one were also sold, to eleven small railways. 24 motor cars and 33 trailers were provided in 1903; on Sundays some motors ran as one-coach trains. Ground-rail pick-up was used, and this was the first railway to operate the Sprague multiple-unit system except experimentally. New stock was added in 1923, 1925, 1936 and 1956. The line passed to BR on nationalisation.

MANCHESTER & MILFORD: this is a high-sounding title for a minor railway, but in fact it only operated between Aberystwyth and Pencader Junction. An early line from near Rhayader on the Mid-Wales was built as far as Llangurig but never opened. Opened from Pencader to Lampeter in 1866 and through to Aberystwyth on 12 Aug. 1867. There were seven engines, 4 0–6–0s, 2 2–4–2Ts, and 1 2–4–0; two of the 0–6–0s were ex-LNW 'coal' engines. The 20 carriages were a mixed collection of 4w., 6w. and bogie; in addition there were some 'Merseys' but probably not owned. The line joined the GWR in 1911, and was closed 22 Feb. 1965.

PORT OF LONDON AUTHORITY: though the PLA lines were mostly goods lines, this undertaking did include two short passenger railways, the London & India Docks Railway and the Millwall Extension Railway. The former was first used for passengers on 3 Aug. 1880, on the 1¾m. from Royal Albert Docks to Gallions. It had a number of goods engines, but the passenger service was worked by ex-LNW 2–4–0Ts, converted from 2–4–0s Nos. 238 (LID 5) 250 (6) and 431 (7), hauling ex-LNW 4w.

carriages. From 1896 the service passed to the GER. The Millwall Extension was also 1¾m. long, from Millwall Junction to North Greenwich, and opened in 1872. At first it was horse-worked with light carriages, (believed to have gone later to the Wisbech & Upwell) as there was a weak swing-bridge. From 1880 three small 2–4–0Ts Nos. 3, 4, 6 from Manning Wardle were used with GER 4w. carriages. The line passed to the PLA in 1909, and the service was later run with three steamcars, two ex-GWR and one ex-Port Talbot Rly. (the only ten-wheeled steamcar). In that connection it is of interest that a steam railcar 'Aeriels Girdle' built in 1851 for the Eastern Counties Railway is said to have worked in its later years for the Millwall Extension Rly. but only after the carriage section had been removed. The line closed to passenger traffic on 2 May 1926.

SOUTH WALES MINERAL RAILWAY (Briton Ferry): this was another railway which operated only a miners' service (Glyncorrwg Colliery) and its history up to incorporation in the GWR in 1908, after a few weeks as officially part of the Port Talbot Rly., is little known. At that time the miners' train comprised 11 old GER 4-wheelers.

TRAFFORD PARK: a public service 3m. from Trafford Road to Barton for people working in the Trafford Park (Manchester) industrial estate was opened in 1897, but as the vehicles used were gas-driven tramcars, it hardly constituted a 'railway' – however in 1908 the cars were worn out, and were replaced by a 0–4–0ST 'Sir William Bailey' (Hudswell Clarke 1908) hauling two ex-Cheshire Lines 4w. carriages; it remained a 'railway' until 1921, when it was pointed out to the Estates Company that it did not have powers to operate passenger trains, and buses were hastily substituted.

Reservoirs

In the great days of reservoir-building, roughly from about 1896 to 1914, there was a need for passenger trains operated by the Water Undertakings, because construction was often being carried out in areas where there were no roads, and vast amounts of cement, stone and bricks were carried up such lines, together with construction workers in second-hand main-line carriages. As described above, one authority (Bradford) obtained a Light Railway Order and ran a proper railway; however most confined their activities to their own requirements, sometimes however taking on through trains from outside, either to show off the works or for a public opening. The following reservoir works were served by substantial standard-gauge lines operating passenger stock: Bamford & Howden, Elan Valley, Ewden Valley, Deepcar, Kinder, Ladybower, Langsett.

Collieries

A number of collieries operated passenger trains for miners over their private lines, sometimes connecting with main lines; in some cases wives and visitors could use the trains, but apart from those in foregoing pages, none were public railways in the proper sense. The trains comprised second-hand carriages from the main lines, hauled by the company's own engines; usually one which was suited to passenger working if available; the Ashington Colliery for instance employed a former LBSCR E1 class 0–6–0T. In the early days there must have been many such services which escaped record; after motor buses became cheaply available from the 'twenties many services ceased, but some continued into the post-1948 era. The following collieries are known to have operated passenger trains:

Aberford (Garforth)
Ashington
Backworth
Blaenserchan
Brereton
Bridgwater (Ashton)
Broomfield
Cannock & Rugeley
Chatterley-Whitfield
Dalton Main
Hazlerigg & Burraton
Kirkheaton
North Walbottle
Powell Duffryn
Shirley
Seaton Burn
Tredegar

Few industrial concerns other than coal-mines had railways with passenger stock other than the odd coach or saloon for special parties. The following did have workmens passenger services for a time; Guest Keen & Nettlefolds, Irlam Soapworks, Manchester Ship Canal, Oxfordshire Ironstone Mines, Port Sunlight complex (Lever Bros), Stewarts & Lloyds (Corby), S. Fox (Stockbridge).

Service Railways

The Army, Navy and Air Force were at one time large users of private railways, and the Army in particular required passenger services at many bases. Again the preference was for second-hand main-line stock; in the early part of the century a considerable number of North London Railway carriages were taken as there was not much else available, but later almost anything could be found in Army bases, in recent years including ex-BR and LTE vehicles. Some vehicles had been shipped abroad for 'campaign' railways and then returned, the best-known being the so-called 'Kitchener' saloon (a rigid eight-wheeler) which contains an incorrect plaque regarding its service in the Sudan (though it was there) and seems to have served at Lydd on its return and later at Shoeburyness. The best-known bases having had standard-gauge passenger services are as follows: Bicester, Bramley, Catterick, Fovant, Longmoor, Lydd, Shoeburyness and Woolwich. The Army also worked the Shropshire & Montgomeryshire railway during the last War, and had passenger stock located at some other points. Several Army railways, such as those to Bisley, Tidworth and Bulford were very extensive, but were worked in conjunction with main-line companies, on the whole with main-line engines stock, though main-line coaches could sometimes be seen paired up with Army locomotives.